Into Thy Word

Into Thy Word

A simple, easy to learn "How To" guide
to better understand the Bible and what
God has to say to us.

Richard Joseph Krejcir

Writer's Showcase
presented by *Writer's Digest*
San Jose New York Lincoln Shanghai

Into Thy Word
A simple, easy to learn "How To" guide to better
understand the Bible and what God has to say to us.

Writer's Showcase
presented by *Writer's Digest*
an imprint of iUniverse.com, Inc.

For information address:
iUniverse.com, Inc.
5220 S 16th, Ste. 200
Lincoln, NE 68512
www.iuniverse.com

ISBN: 0-595-14873-5

Printed in the United States of America

DEDICATION

I dedicate this work to the GLORY OF OUR LORD!

"I have been crucified with Christ and I no longer live, but Christ lives in me. The life I live in the body, I live by faith in the Son of God, who loved me and gave himself for me." {Gal. 2:20}

Many thanks to all the people who have discipled and inspired me over the years, such as Steve Morgan, Chuck Miller, R.C. Sproul, and Robert B. Munger.

And of course my great love and appreciation to my love for all of her help, my wife MaryRuth, "*I found the one my heart loves*" Song of Solomon 3:4

"I learned years ago to go to the place for the deepest lessons of life. That one place is the Bible." R.A. Torrey

Epigraph

"This book contains the mind of God, the state of man, the way of salvation, the doom of sinners, and the happiness of believers. Its doctrines are holy, its precepts are binding, its histories are true, and its decisions are immutable. Read it to be wise, believe in it to be safe, and practice it to be holy. It contains light to direct you, food to support you, and comfort to cheer you. It is the traveler's map, the pilgrim's staff, the pilot's compass, the soldier's sword, and the Christian's charter. Here paradise is restored, heaven opened, and the gates of hell disclosed. Christ is its grand object, our good its design, and the glory of God its end. It should fill the memory, rule the heart, and guide the feet. Read it slowly, frequently, and prayerfully. It is a mine of wealth, a paradise of glory, and a river of pleasure. It is given you in life, will be opened in the judgment, and be remembered forever. It involves the highest responsibility, will reward the greatest labor, and will condemn all who trifle with its sacred contents."

—-Author Unknown

CONTENTS

FORWARD

This book is about getting the non-Christian to learn how to study the Bible, and this book is for the Pastor and theologian who needs to have their "refresh" button pressed. This book is in fact for anybody desiring to know the Book of ages. If you are new to the Word or are a seasoned teacher. If you do not know where to begin, or you have tried countless times and feel overwhelmed and frustrated, this is the book for you!

Some people view the Bible as an un-climbable mountain, a dark cave that is feared to be trespassed upon. Be encouraged, and be comforted, that you can indeed do it. You can climb that mountain and venture into the cave with confidence. In fact you will be able to mine the truths as an expert "exegete" does! The Bible is a diamond mine filled with precious nuggets that can be applied to your life, for a life to be transformed and renewed! As with any mine you do have to start digging in it before you will find the diamonds, and the more you dig the more you will find!

This book was conceived back in 1979. I was a new Christian and was teaching a "campaigners" Bible study at a "Young Life" group. I was in High school myself and was frustrated that all the books on how to study the Bible were too technical and few. I felt there was no better subject to teach than how to study God's Word yourself, so I embarked on a research project that has spanned for over 20 years, to find the best ways to get into Thy Word. At first it was a couple sheets of paper with tips, then a booklet, and it grew and grew. I kept refining, condensing, while striving to keep it simple and easy to understand.

I have taught these truths to Junior High and High School groups, Singles groups, Camps and Conferences and even older adults. It is my call and passion that you learn for yourself the most negated aspect of the Christian Life, THE BIBLE! It may be the greatest best seller of all time hundreds of times over, but is perhaps the least read book in the Christian's home. Let us turn that trend around, blow off the dust and dive into the greatest adventure ever conceived.

In His Service

Richard
Nub. 6:24

PREFACE

This is a simple guide to help you dig into God's Word. These steps you are about to embark upon are not difficult. In fact they are quite easy, there are no elaborate condescending methods, just a common sense approach to get all we can from God's most precious Word. I first developed this study over 15 years ago, and have taught it to countless groups from Junior Highers to Pastors. I carefully honed it and it has become very practical and beneficial.

Just like learning a new compute program, there is a learning curve, even when the program is easier. Remember the old days of computers, learning all those "DOS" commands. Now we just scroll the mouse and click. This book will allow you to scroll and click with ease. These "steps" will become second nature like a seasoned pastor spends a fraction of the time in his sermon preparation than when he first came out of seminary. You too can become a "pro" into God's Word!

This book is for the new Christian, who has never picked up a Bible before and for the seasoned Bible teacher to be refreshed, because we all still need to be learning and growing. Besides an old dog can pick up some new tricks!

The primary purpose is to show you "How" in a logical clear and concise way to study His Word. This guide is not an exhaustive scholarly endeavor. There are many works that fit that bill, but they are not for the average Christian. They tend to be so technical that people will buy the book, but soon give up with it, and thus give up with knowing the Bible deeper.

This Guide will provide you with the "map" of questions, tools, and a chart; but you must provide the will. To surrender our will to God's will is the essential element of being a growing Christian. God's Word provides the way; you simply provide the means.

There are many ways we can study the Bible effectively. There is no "best" way, only that we do it! Many Christians feel all they have to do for Bible lessons is sit in a pew, turn on the television or radio, or naturally receive their knowledge for being a Christian; but this is not how to transform our lives. We must read and get into the Word of God ourselves: Through prayer, hard work, discipline, concentration, application, and even more **prayer!**

"For the Word of God is quick and powerful, and sharper than any two edged sword, piercing even to the dividing asunder of soul and spirit, and the joints and marrow, and is discerner of the thoughts and intents of the heart."
{Hebrews 4:12 KJV}

So set aside time each day free from distractions and go for it with passion and vigor. As you start to dive into these steps and gain more insights into His marvelous Word, you will find your life transformed; not because of this book, because of His book. You will find a growing sense of anticipation as you approach your study time, and that the study of His Word becomes fun and enjoyable. You will discover more in a few minutes than what you ever did before. You will find that over an hour of your "old" way of just reading it like a textbook will no longer reveal the results that these "pointers" will in a fraction of the time!

• **So let Christ transform you through His Word.**

LIST OF ABBREVIATIONS

[All scripture references will be from the "New International Version" by Zondervan Publishing House 1973, 1978, 1984 unless otherwise noted]

Additional Scriptural abbreviations are listed in Appendix B.

Part I

INTO THY WORD WORKBOOK.

This is designed for the individual to go through to better understand how to dig into God's Word. Part II will be a "curriculum" that can be used in a group study, or individually to further challenge you.

CHAPTER I

"PRELUDE INTO GOD'S TREASURE CHEST"

"At that time Jesus said, "I praise you, Father, Lord of heaven and earth, because you have hidden these things from the wise and learned, and revealed them to little children."
{Matt. 11:25}

Before we can effectively venture into His Word we must ask ourselves; Do you call yourself an expert on receivership? You probably say what !?! Or no way! But do you live your life with having a "me first" identity, always placing the emphases on the "I" and "Me". If only I…If it could go this way for me…Then I could….So that the ownership of your life is completely self-focused and centered. The ownership of your life is yours and yours alone! But Christ calls us to Him, and out of ourselves. Our ownership has been transferred, our pink slip has been signed over from ourselves to Christ, If you claim Christ as your Lord. What effect are you having to those around you? And how well are you getting into His Word? When we release ourselves to Christ, then the proper attitude of life will take over. The vision of our life and the result of what we have will be based on a positive outlook. A positive attitude that is based solely on what Christ has done for us. So regardless of our external circumstances we are to be totally focused on our Lord. We then are to allow our attitudes to be Christ centered. We could allow our circumstances to take the lead or Christ to take the lead, the choice is given to us, but beware of the consequences.

If we are receivership oriented and not Christ centered, then all of those circumstances will be squeezed, and bitterness and resentment will flow out of them. Or we can be Christ centered and oils of sweetness will pour out. What pours out from you? The love and care that is modeled to those around us or bitterness and hostility. Now know that bitterness will not be squeezed from our circumstances, but from our attitude that results from those circumstances. The way Christ is exhibited in you will be from your focus and attitude and not your circumstances. Your direction in life, your joy and happiness, your cares and concerns, your willingness to reach beyond yourself will grow from your attitude and maturity, all stemming from who you are in Christ!

Then the circumstance will change once we realize our wrong thinking and error and the receivership mentality dies within us, and the Christ centered life is birthed. This is the way we are made, the reason we endure suffering, the way a fallen sinful and unjust world is turned from the glory of Satan into the glory of our Lord. By allowing Christ to reach in us and conform us to His image and character, regardless of what we are going through, regardless of our circumstances. As we raise up Christ up in our thinking, in our attitude, so that it changes who we are and what we do. So that we are people of distinction by our perceived behavior by others from a changed core of who we are by what Christ has done!

The attitude will be the impact that strikes at the issues of life. That will allow us to get into His Word effectively and passionately with out the primary obstacle of wrong attitude in the way. Breaking away from our hurt and pain to the absorption of grace and the acceptance of Christ will allow our growth and impact to expand. We cannot trust in our education, wealth, success, failures, people, appearances, skill, Spiritual Gifts, or circumstances. The attitude of trusting in things and circumstances must be laid on the floor of the cross and no where else. So the attitude of trust in Christ takes over who we are. Our attitude must be Christ driven and not appearances driven. We must embrace the day with joy, knowing Christ is at work in us, in those around us.

Life is 10% what happens to us and 90% how we react to it. As the elect, saved by grace, it is still up to us what we make out of what Christ gives us. Maturity will make the difference of a life of distinction and purpose, or a life governed by strife and stress. So what is your response, what is your attitude were does your maturity lay?

ATTITUDE: *"I have been crucified with Christ and I no longer live, but Christ lives in me. The life I live in the body, I live by faith in the Son of God, who loved me and gave himself for me."* {Gal. 2:20}

Start with the proper attitude! Our minds must be clear and childlike before Him, because when you read His Word you are before the face of God! You are going before a Holy God, so adjust yourself with these attitudes:

➤ *REVERENCE: "But the LORD is in his holy temple; let all the earth be silent before him."* {Hab. 2:20, Psalm 89:7}

Prepare your heart and mind. You are not going to a football game! Be quiet; clear your distracting thoughts and desires away!

➤ *YOUR WILL: "My son, if you accept my words and store up my commands within you, turning your ear to wisdom and applying your heart to understanding, and if you call out for insight and cry aloud for understanding, and if you look for it as for silver and search for it as for hidden treasure, then you will understand the fear of the LORD and find the knowledge of God."* { Prov. 2:1-5}

"Sanctify them by the truth; your word is truth..." {John 7:17f}

We must be willing to not only read but to obey God's decrees! It is not about you, it is about God! Make it your choice and work hard with a surrendered will to His!

➢ *ANTICIPATION: "O God, you are my God, earnestly I seek you; my soul thirsts for you, my body longs for you, in a dry and weary land where there is no water."* {Psalm 63:1}

We must come before God with eagerness and expectancy. This is not a chore; it is fellowship with the Creator of the universe, what better time could there be!

➢ *BE ALERT: "The fear of the LORD is the beginning of knowledge, but fools despise wisdom and discipline;" "Trust in the LORD with all your heart and lean not on your own understanding."* {Prov. 1:7; 3:5-6}

Find a time where you are most alert and awake!

➢ *BE IN LOVE: "I have not departed from the commands of his lips; I have treasured the words of his mouth more than my daily bread;" "When your words came, I ate them; they were my joy and my heart's delight, for I bear your name, O LORD God Almighty."* {Job 23:12; Jeremiah. 15:16}

Fall in love with His Word! Have the appetite, as it was better than your favorite meal! Do not let it be just a duty! The love will increase as we increase in our effort and study!

In God's eyes it is far more important **why** we do something rather than that we do something, even good.

"Do not consider his appearance or his height, for I have rejected him. The LORD does not look at the things man looks at. Man looks at the outward appearance, but the LORD looks at the heart;" "He did what was right in the eyes of the LORD, but not wholeheartedly."
{I Sam 16:7, II Chron. 25:2}

Thus we do not want to do the right thing with the wrong attitude and motives.

"Open my eyes that I may see wonderful things in your law." {Psalm 119:18}

A very important point: For this to work you must have a relationship with Christ, with your trust in His grace. Without it, you are programming a computer without any knowledge of its language or design. You may attempt it, but all you will get is *gibberish, "foolishness,"* as Scripture tells us, the knowledge will be hidden from you.

"The man without the Spirit does not accept the things that come from the Spirit of God, for they are foolishness to him, and he cannot understand them, because they are spiritually discerned. The spiritual man makes judgments about all things, but he himself is not subject to any man's judgment." {I Cor. 14-15}

"GETTING STARTED" TO VENTURE INTO THY WORD

"Remember the Morning watch," was the rallying cry on the Cambridge University campus in 1882. Several students intended on growing deeper in their faith at a time when the popularity of Godly devotion was being replaced by scientific and liberal thinking. These students decided to take a stand in adversity and academic backlash.

Their lives would echo as they do today on our public high school and college campuses. They found the harsh reality that Christianity was not an academic pursuit, instead filling their schedules with lectures, sporting events, studies, and student gatherings and so forth, just like we do today, but without TV!

The students found a fatal flaw in their busyness, even though they made a commitment to honor Christ: They had little time for the One they were honoring! As they described *"A crack in our spiritual armor, if not closed will bring us disaster!"*

So they sought an answer to their dilemma, a scheme to balance the hectic schedules and honor God. They came up with a plan called "The Morning Watch," that for the first few minutes of the day will be dedicated to know the Lord.

One of the young men who was not fond of mornings devised a mechanical contraption with all kinds of levers and pulleys to persuade him out of bed!

This idea spread like a wild fire and was used by God for a revival in England, which was depicted in the film "Chariots of Fire." The modern missionary movement was born as many Evangelical Ministries still in existence today, such as YMCA and the Boy Scouts. Many famous pastors and missionaries who influenced many generations all stemming from giving God the first fruits of your day.

So will you meet this challenge?

The Challenge is simple, the idea is pure and practical, and only requires your obedience and persistence! God desires our intimacy, our relationship, and our communion with His holiness. Wow what an honor and opportunity to go before the holy Creator of the universe.

"Listen to my cry for help, my King and my God, for to you I pray. In the morning, O LORD, you hear my voice; in the morning I lay my requests before you and wait in expectation." "My heart is steadfast, O God, my

heart is steadfast; I will sing and make music. Awake, my soul! Awake, harp and lyre! I will awaken the dawn." Psalm 5:2-3; 57:7

So I challenge you to set aside time each day, the best time you have when you are the most alert and able to go before your creator and redeemer.

If you are a new Christian desiring to know how to read the Bible or if you have been away from it for a while. If you have not ever been discipled or never really put in the time and effort into the "Walk with Christ," then get ready to start. It is never too late, unless you die!

The following "7-UP" guide is an excellent way to start your new life in Christ, or renew yourself and get back on track!!! I first learned of this while attending "Navigators" {a Christian outreach Bible study committed to discipleship on the college campus} meetings when I was in college.

Start it off simple, say 7 minutes, and you can call it "7-UP!" Seven minutes a day, seven days a week.

First pray for guidance, and prepare your heart and mind, take 1/2 a minute. Tell God how much you love Him. This is worship!

Second read a passage from God's Word, and spend at least 4 minutes. That can be just a couple of chapters.

Do not know where to start? Start with the book of John. Or get a hold of the "The One Year Bible" from Tyndale. It has a passage from the Old Testament, the New Testament, as well as a Psalm and Proverb that takes you through the whole Bible in a year. {This is reading at a rate of 15 minutes a day. To start out, cut it in half, and you are on track for 7-up.} You can also read half when you wake up and half when you go to bed to start off with. Or create your own schedule, just keep it up! **If you are new to God's Word or have been away from it for a while, get the "New Living Translation." It is easy to read and understand.**

Third spend the rest of the 2 1/2 minutes in specific prayer. Such as your parents/family, school/work, people in your life, confession of your sins, and what you are thankful for. You may add the problems of our society, or spend it in silence and reverent meditation over the passage you just read, and that's it!

Then as you progress, you will have the desire to spend even more time. Most committed Christians will spend more than an hour in prayer each day plus time in scripture. You say you do not have the time? Well many Christian leaders do it and they have schedules that would blow yours away!

There is always time, the question is will you make it?

So when the morning watch comes....

What will you do?

CHAPTER II

"THE WHY OF BIBLE STUDY"

"We present you this book, the most valuable thing that this world affords. Here is the wisdom; this is the royal law; these are the lively oracles of God." {The coronation of Queen Elizabeth, as she was given a Bible.}

Too often most people will dismiss the Bible as an antiquated book of rhetoric, which has no meaning for us in our modern age. They believe that the Bible was responsible for the problems of darkness and disgust of ages past. Even Christians who carry her under their arms to church, may never venture into her pages, thus an insult may occur to their will and intellect.

Yet the Bible has always been true. We may attempt to dismiss its claims and its intrusion into our lives. However the Bible has been the light in darkness, the strength in our weakness, our comfort in our troubles, and our guide for our life. Because God's Word is, *"more precious than gold, than much pure gold; and is more sweeter than honey."* {Psalm 19:10}

When we try to live the Christian life alone without the guidance and support from the Word, we are like a pilot of an airplane flying through thick clouds totally confused. A pilot who then refuses to admit that they have vertigo {where you are disoriented and have no clue what direction you are going or even if you are upside down!} and continues to fly upside down!

- As a Christian, we need to live a life of distinction, and the only way to receive the knowledge of that distinction is to get into the Word!

- We do not want to be "bar-code" Christians who do not care what's in the box only the label matters, or that Christianity is just "fire insurance" from hell!

We must seek out the truth and answers that we need, from the final authority, and not the ways of the world! If not then we set up ourselves as the final judge and authority and not God, thus we will lead ourselves to hell from false truths and distractions.

The point of Christianity is to be a transformed person, through self-surrender to our Lord's holiness through His Word and prayer!

The Response of grace is to be a transformed person, through self-surrender to our Lord's holiness through His Word and prayer!

REMEMBER: *THE BIBLE IS GOD'S LOVE LETTER TO YOU!!!*

- We need to get into the Bible ourselves. One of the problems of Christianity today is that we are conditioned to be taught from the scriptures but not to do it for ourselves.

- The cults place their authority elsewhere, and not in the Word!

THE STUDY OF THE BIBLE MATTERS!

Because it brings us inline to His Holiness, and with reality! Science may have explanations, but they change completely every few years, however the Word of God never changes, what a great comfort!

Science can never explain love, justice, peace, goodness, purity, sin...because you cannot quantify it in a microscope or scientific instrument! "Why we do what we do," cannot be scientifically measured and hypothesized, that is why there are so many theories in science and psychology and they are always changing!

- The Bible is read much, but studied little!

- The truths of Scripture will transcend any other subject, discipline or passion!

The Bible gives us a greater reality that can not be seen but is clearly felt, and to deny it is like living in Huntington Beach in Southern California and never seeing the ocean!

BECAUSE?

➤ Because the Bible is a "SWORD" *"For the word of God is living and active. Sharper than any double-edged sword, it penetrates even to dividing soul and spirit, joints and marrow; it judges the thoughts and attitudes of the heart."* {Heb. 4:12}

The Bible is living and powerful. Thus Jesus is living, Jesus is sharp and will cut and penetrate our hearts. It will open us up from the inside out to reveal our nakedness and impurity!

➢ Since the Bible is a sword, it is a weapon that can and will defeat the dark forces against us, so we must know it to be able to use it! *"Take the helmet of salvation and the sword of the Spirit, which is the word of God."* {Eph. 6:17}

➢ Because the Bible is a "TACTICAL WEAPON" *"so is my word that goes out from my mouth: It will not return to me empty, but will accomplish what I desire and achieve the purpose for which I sent it."* {Isaiah 55:11}

You can aim the Bible for specific purposes.

➢ Because the Bible is a "SEED." *"So that, they may be ever seeing but never perceiving, and ever hearing but never understanding; otherwise they might turn and be forgiven!"* {Mark 4:1-9}

A small but powerful word can make a big miracle in the heart and actions of the Bible student. And will only grow under the right soil conditions of His Spirit not in our will!

➢ Because the Bible is a "MIRROR." *"Therefore, get rid of all moral filth and the evil that is so prevalent and humbly accept the word planted in you, which can save you. Do not merely listen to the word, and so deceive yourselves. Do what it says. Anyone who listens to the word but does not do what it says is like a man who looks at his face in a mirror and, after looking at himself, goes away and immediately forgets what he looks like. But the man who looks intently into the perfect law that gives freedom, and continues to do this, not forgetting what he has heard, but doing it—he will be blessed in what he does."* {James 1:21-25}

The Bible will reflect what is in our hearts and minds! It will show you the truth. Will you accept it?

➢ Because the Bible is a "ROCK." *"Therefore everyone who hears these words of mine and puts them into practice is like a wise man who built his house on the rock. The rain came down, the streams rose, and the winds blew and beat against that house; yet it did not fall, because it had its foundation on the rock. But everyone who hears these words of mine and does not put them into practice is like a foolish man who built his house on sand. The rain came down, the streams rose, and the winds blew and beat against that house, and it fell with a great crash."* {Matt 7:24-27}

The Bible is the foundation for our life and work. Without it, we are building on sand that will wash us away! Without it we will be unable to withstand the pressures of life and the call Christ gives us! It is essential in building anything relevant and purposeful.

➢ Because the Bible is "LIVING WATER." *"The Samaritan woman said to him, You are a Jew and I am a Samaritan woman. How can you ask me for a drink?" (For Jews do not associate with Samaritans.) Jesus answered her, "If you knew the gift of God and who it is that asks you for a drink, you would have asked him and he would have given you living water." "Sir, the woman said, you have nothing to draw with and the well is deep. Where can you get this living water? Are you greater than our father Jacob, who gave us the well and drank from it himself, as did also his sons and his flocks and herds? Jesus answered, Everyone who drinks this water will be thirsty again, but whoever drinks the water I give him will never thirst. Indeed, the water I give him will become in him a spring of water welling up to eternal life."* {John 4:9-14}

The Bible is the fountain we are to drink from!

➢ Because the Bible is our "BREAD." *"Therefore, rid yourselves of all malice and all deceit, hypocrisy, envy, and slander of every kind. Like newborn babies, crave pure spiritual milk, so that by it you may grow up in your salvation, now that you have tasted that the Lord is good."* {I Pet 2:1-3}

The Bible is our spiritual food, and we are what we eat!

➢ Because the Bible is the record of God speaking!

- We cannot believe and trust in Christ without the knowledge from the Bible, because it is our primary source material.

- If the Bible is in doubt, then all of our faith rests in mud and has no foundation to stand on, that is why a high view of scripture is essential to the growing believer!

As you can see the Word of God is essential to our function as a Christian. It is essential to our understanding of not only God, but ourselves as well. Without God's Word we will be purposeless and disrupted from our call and the purpose for our salvation. When we base our lives on the Word of God, then Christ can create His work in us by the power of the Spirit!

▪ VALUE IS A MATTER OF WORTH, SO WHAT IS IT WORTH TO YOU?

"So What" you say?

- The Bible brings us into the reality of life!

- The world is a material temporary entity. We are being formed for eternity! That is this life is a mere rehearsal for the main performance and its many stays for the life to come.

- The Bible is a greater reality than what is seen!

SO FIND OUT FOR YOURSELVES!!!

- The Bible calls us to faith and accountability in its entirety, and to have faith in it without risk {since our place is already secured in heaven!} and with trust in any situation we encounter.

- The Bible is reliable and stands the test of time, so is your trust there or elsewhere?

- The Bible is the reliable source of historical information, the record of God speaking!

- The Bible is the source for our contact and guidance with our creator!

- The Bible is our story, our history, our struggles, our opportunities, our hope and the climax of His plan and redemption.

- The Bible tells who we are and what we are, it gives us purpose and meaning, and our response is how we choose to live.

- The Bible is our source for life and liberty and happiness!

- The Bible is our secure mast on the boat of life, struggling in its way through the storms of the world. It is our firm foundation, which we need to grip tightly.

The Bible is not to be a secret, but shared and communicated with power and conviction, because it has been entrusted to us as bearers of, as agents of, and witness of it's truth!

- **This will give you greater personal conviction,** *"I want to know Christ and the power of his resurrection and the fellowship of sharing in his sufferings, becoming like him in his death."*{Phil. 3:10})!

- **Your life will change** *"In the beginning was the Word, and the Word was with God, and the Word was God. He was with God in the beginning. Through him all things were made; without him nothing was made that has been made."* {John 1:1-3}!

- **Your attitudes will change** *"I have written you in my letter not to associate with sexually immoral people—not at all meaning the people of this world who are immoral, or the greedy and swindlers, or idolaters. In that case you would have to leave this world."* {I Cor. 5:9-10}!

- **You will be pointed in the right direction,** *"but those who hope in the LORD will renew their strength. They will soar on wings like eagles; they will run and not grow weary, they will walk and not be faint."* {Isaiah 40:31}!

- **The glory of God will be pointed out to you,** *"Ah, Sovereign LORD,"* I said, *"I do not know how to speak; I am only a child..."* {Jeremiah 1:6f}!

- The Bible will break through our self-will and deceptions including sin and temptations and rationalizations, because the Bible is the voice of God! *"I hope you will put up with a little of my foolishness; but you are already doing that…"* {II Cor 11:1f}

- The temptation of Jesus was to satisfy His physical hunger, but His focus was the Father!

- There is no other final authority than the Word of God!

REMEMBER: THE BIBLE CHANGES LIVES!!!

- You will become a greater person by being a greater servant.

- Your message and witness will be increased greatly.

- Bible study reveals real life principles for us all. Our problems and struggles become minor shadows to His glory!

The promise of scripture is that it may not promise us riches and problem free lives, what it does promise is His presence. When we place our trust in Christ because of His Word to guide us, then we will have lives enriched with purpose, meaning and fulfillment.

"Do not let this Book of the Law depart from your mouth; meditate on it day and night, so that you may be careful to do everything written in it. Then you will be prosperous and successful." {Joshua 1:8}

Checkout Proverbs 1 and Psalm 1

- Ask the Lord to give you strength and perseverance in discipleship, to remain true to your calling and opportunities He has for you!

- Let us not forget the results of placing Christ first in our lives! *"I have hidden your word in my heart that I might not sin against you;" "Your word is a lamp to my feet and a light for my path."* {Psalm 119:11;105}

Checkout John 8:31-36; 15:11; 16:33; 17:17

THE MAIN GOAL OF BIBLE STUDY:

DON'T JUST INTERPRET IT, BUT APPLY IT TO YOUR LIFE!!!

Unfortunately a lot of Christians think that all we have to do is read the Bible, and do what it says, and there is nothing to interpret. Or they will react against the educated "professional" Christian who is a teacher, scholar or pastor. They see that person taking the Bible away from them, and wrapping it in confusion. They do not want the Bible to be some kind of obscure book they cannot understand. But what they are in fact doing is reading the Bible without any understanding and making excuses for it and it is very doubtful they are doing what it says! {Of course some scholar's love to wrap things in confusion!}

- Some Christians have no problems with interpretation, it is the application and obedience that they have trouble with. We tend to understand the precepts of the Bible so well that we will rationalize them away, such as *"do everything without complaining or arguing"* {Phil. 2:14}. Thus we complain and argue all the time.

- The primary goal of interpretation is to find the "plain meaning" of the Bible!

REMEMBER: BE SURE TO INCORPORATE WHAT YOU KNOW INTO YOUR LIFE!!!

- It is not enough TO KNOW something; but we must be able TO DO something, this is what our response to grace and sanctification is about!

There are too many people in the world who just do not get it! Just as the Pharisees asked Jesus for a miracle after He fed over 4,000 people! Just as some crazy guy was screaming at the airport ticket person to get on his flight after they announced the airport is closed due to fog. Just as so many Christians sit in their pews every Sunday and do nothing for the Lord; they just do not get it! {Mark 8}
One of the great things about the Bible is it is honest with the characters that it portrays. If we were to write such a book, would we explain our weakness and stupidity, or how great we are? The Bible reveals the good, the bad, and the ugly, and it will with us too!

"You search the scriptures because you believe they give you eternal life. But the Scriptures point to me." {John 5:39}

The question is do we get it? Since the Bible is God's authoritative Word, we no doubt will spend more time in it! Are we prepared to allow the Word of God to get in us and make changes and to transform and renew our minds for His glory? {Romans 12}

- If the Bible is not where you place your trust, then where is your trust and where will it lead you?

- We cannot have the Words of Jesus without the Bible!

- The Bible is the chariot that carries the voice of God!

We as the people of God who have been saved from our sins by the grace of our Lord Jesus Christ have a call, a mandate: to preserve His Word, and to proclaim His Word. We must remain steadfast in this call to our individual selves, as well as our neighbor.

"We must pay more careful attention, therefore, to what we have heard, so that we do not drift away. For if the message spoken by angels was binding, and every violation and disobedience received its just punishment, how shall we escape if we ignore such a great salvation? {Heb. 2:1-3}

A word about all those different versions, and translations:

Remember the Bible was written in Hebrew for most of the Old Testament, and Greek for the New Testament. So there is always many ways to translate a different language.

You can do it literally such as the "NASB" word for word, or as close as possible while keeping it readable such as the "NIV." And you can translate it in a contemporary language so it is easy to read such as the "Contemporary English version," or the "New Century Version" or "The Message." But they are being loose to the original language, thus are paraphrases and lose some of the real literal meaning. They are good for reading through the Bible to get to know it, but for serious Bible study you need the "NASB" "The New King James Version" or the "NIV." [See Appendix B]

So which one should I read?

I recommend the "New International Version" {NIV} as your main Bible for study, and the "New living Translation" {NLT} for devotions. Then you can choose either the "The New King James Version" {NKJV} or the "New American Standard Bible" {NASB} to compare with. And one or more of the paraphrases, my favorite is the "Contemporary English version" {CEV} and the "New living Translation," they are excellent for getting to know the Word and for daily devotions! So you will have at least 3 translations, you can also get a "Parallel Bible" that lists several translations side by side.

NOW WHAT? NOW I KNOW WHY; WHAT DO I DO?

So how do we study the Bible? Countless copies of scripture are sold and sit on shelves and bookcases unread! Why? Because people do not know how to engage it, how to read the Word of our Lord: Too apprehensive with fear of conviction or unsure how to go about it.

Yet God himself gives us the directions and the ability to proceed.

"Ask and it will be given to you; seek and you will find; knock and the door will be opened to you. For everyone who asks receives; he who seeks finds; and to him who knocks, the door will be opened." {Matt 7:7}

"He who does not love me will not obey my teaching. These words you hear are not my own; they belong to the Father who sent me." {John 14:24}

"If any of you lacks wisdom, he should ask God, who gives generously to all without finding fault, and it will be given to him." {James 1:25}

We can make the Bible real in our lives, so let us not be filled with fear or with apprehension; but, put our discouragement away with confidence that we can go before God by the power of His Spirit, through His Word!

So jump in and envelop yourself into the study of God's Word. You may start off with Genesis or with Matthew or John. You may want to do a little Old Testament and New Testament each time in which case I recommend the "One Year Bible" by Tyndale.

The following is a simple seven- (7) step process to grow in God's Word. This is designed for you to get the most out of your studies. By focusing on His Word firsthand, then the power and transformation that the early Christians had can be yours! Then you can have the life of a disciple, a life transformed by the work of our Lord, and applying the Bible to your life.

"He called you to this through our gospel, that you might share in the glory of our Lord Jesus Christ. So then, brothers, stand firm and hold to the teachings we passed on to you, whether by word of mouth or by letter." {II Thess. 2:14-15}

CHAPTER III

"STEP I": KNOWING THE KNOWABLE

BRINGING OUR MIND TO BE RIGHT WITH GOD!

"Therefore, I urge you, brothers, in view of God's mercy, to offer your bodies as living sacrifices, holy and pleasing to God—this is your spiritual act of worship. Do not conform any longer to the pattern of this world, but be transformed by the renewing of your mind. Then you will be able to test and approve what God's will is—his good, pleasing and perfect will. For by the grace given me I say to every one of you: Do not think of yourself more highly than you ought, but rather think of yourself with sober judgment, in accordance with the measure of faith God has given you." {Romans 12:1-3}

If we do not have the right attitude and mindset, you will not get much out of God's Word, because your will is in the way of His!

The Word of God will not allow us to stumble in the dark and be the straw that blows in the wind, dependent on the whims and trends of our culture.

By knowing the knowable will keep us centered on what is right and true in a world that has lost its direction and compass. The world's relativism and materialism that has rejected truth and God will not capture us who place our trust in Christ. And our trust will gain momentum and growth through His Word.

Now that you have established a constant devotional time with God that includes Bible reading and prayer, you will find yourself hungering for More! That is the Holy Spirit working in you, desiring you to grow in Him! Desiring you to dive deeper and more earnestly into His Word. These "steps" are in stages from beginner to more advanced and so forth. As you advance in your faith and practice, then each stage will help prepare and challenge you to grow closer in our Love relationship with our Lord Jesus Christ.

- We all are beginners, do not skip "stages" thinking you already know it, because we do not always know what we think we know!

FIRST: PRAYER!!! *"Open my eyes that I may see wonderful things in your law."* {Psalm 119:18}

This is the essential first step, to always, always start anything especially studying the Bible with communication to God!

- Do not just open up in a short quip of prayer, be in a state of prayer from the time you open the Book of God until you close the cover.

- No microscope or scientific instrument will open up the wonders and meanings more than prayer.

- You are before the Holiness of God when you are in His Word. So be in continual prayer through your entire time of study and reading.

"If any of you lacks wisdom, he should ask God, who gives generously to all without finding fault, and it will be given to him. But when he asks, he

must believe and not doubt, because he who doubts is like a wave of the sea, blown and tossed by the wind." {James 1:5-6}

- We must be in tune with the author to be able to understand His book!

SECOND: DIRECT YOUR WILL AND SEIZE THE OPPORTUNITY!!!

We must submit to the authority of Scripture, even if it goes against our experience and perceptions, and especially if it goes against our will. We cannot have a growing and mature relationship in Christ without being discipled, and we cannot be discipled without being submissive. Tough to do in our culture, but a must for us to do, to be all we can be for His glory!

"Whoever has my commands and obeys them, he is the one who loves me. He who loves me will be loved by my Father, and I too will love him and show myself to him. Then Judas (not Judas Iscariot) said, But, Lord, why do you intend to show yourself to us and not to the world? Jesus replied, If anyone loves me, he will obey my teaching. My Father will love him, and we will come to him and make our home with him. He who does not love me will not obey my teaching. These words you hear are not my own; they belong to the Father who sent me." {John 14:21-24}

What is discipleship? It is the growing commitment by the power of the Holy Spirit, which is a lifestyle rooted in Christ: Christ as our Lord, and not just a Savior. That means we are not lords of our manor, or even of ourselves, rather Christ is our King. This is also what worship is, giving Christ our best through praise and thanksgiving.

- This means that our will is surrendered to the Lordship of Christ as our King!

- Pray to the Lord and ask Him to become more "real" to you!

- When we realize who we are in Christ, how "real" He is, then our trust and obedience becomes more constant and continual!

You have to make a commitment and stick to it. By sticking to it will allow you to become more motivated and constant, thus the more you do, the easier it becomes!

"If, while we seek to be justified in Christ, it becomes evident that we ourselves are sinners, does that mean that Christ promotes sin? Absolutely not! If I rebuild what I destroyed, I prove that I am a lawbreaker. For through the law I died to the law so that I might live for God. I have been crucified with Christ and I no longer live, but Christ lives in me. The life I live in the body, I live by faith in the Son of God, who loved me and gave himself for me. I do not set aside the grace of God, for if righteousness could be gained through the law, Christ died for nothing!" {Gal. 2: 17-21}

- If not we become the disgruntled "pew-sitter" who gossips and complains out of arrogance and apathy, who models the rotten aspects of life to the world in the name of Christ!

Make the Bible a habit! Psychologists tell us it can take over 40 days for an action to become a habit. So be patient and invest the time, and do not expect instant results. Gifted mature Christians have spent decades studying it! So do not give up! Do not be like most people who give up after a few days or weeks!

- **Make a VOW, A Commitment.** *"For I resolved to know nothing while I was with you except Jesus Christ and him crucified."* {I Cor. 2:2}

Take the initiative! Be constant and continual, do not expect great grand slams off the first pitches, as with anything, it takes time!

- **You must have the desire.** *"Blessed are those who hunger and thirst after righteousness, for they shall be filled."* {Mat 5:6}

- **Pick a Good Time.** *"Very early in the morning, while it was still dark, Jesus got up, left the house and went off to a solitary place, where he prayed."* {Mk 1:35}

When you are the most alert and at your best. If you are not a night person then do not do it then! We need to give God the best part of our day, and not our leftovers! Sometimes it is best to split it in two, like morning and evening. **BE CONSISTENT!!!** Whatever the time: And do not stand God up!

Remember the Morning Watch. *"Satisfy us in the morning with your unfailing love, that we may sing for joy and be glad all our days."* {Psalm 90:14}

Most Christians through the centuries gave God that time! Because that is when we are usually most alert and uncluttered with the days activities.

If you start off halfheartedly you will fail!

You must allow the reading of the Word to be securely rooted in who you are as a person. Tell others what you are doing so they can hold you accountable!

"See that what you have heard from the beginning remains in you. If it does, you also will remain in the Son and in the Father. And this is what he promised us—even eternal life." {I John 2:24-25}

- Know for certain and be encouraged that you can do it, you can stand firm in the Word, you can be transformed!!!

THIRD: LOGGING TIME

- **Spend time** keeping the Bible "Dusted" by reading and re-reading it!

- **Make a commitment** on how much you will read. Use a chart or a notebook to see your progress. If you just do it occasionally, you will receive benefit, but not as much as you would being constant.

See Appendix D for a Bible reading chart.

RELAX! *"Be still, and know that I am God; I will be exalted among the nations, I will be exalted in the earth."* {Psalm 46:10}

Quiet Yourself and spend a little time waiting on God, listening. Do NOT rush into God's Word! Do not be in a hurry! Do not race through the Word of God! And do not bite off more than you can chew, reading more than you can.

"Search me, O God, and know my heart; test me and know my anxious thoughts. See if there is any offensive way in me, and lead me in the way everlasting." {PSALM 139:23-24}

SET GOALS FOR YOURSELF:

- Make a commitment to how much time you will spend. I suggest starting off at 15 minutes after mastering the "7-UP" minutes and then build up. Do not start too much or you will burn out! Most mature Christians spend over 1 hour a day.

- 15 minutes in the morning, 15 minutes at lunch, and 15 minutes before bed will = 45 minutes. {You have 168 hours in a week, how much will belong to God?}

- Make a commitment when you will read: **For example:** Start off in the morning and then again in the evening, and slowly start to increase the time. Do not watch the clock, stay focused!

REMEMBER: Quality is more important then Quantity!

- **Have a Special Place.** *"Early the next morning Abraham got up and returned to the place where he had stood before the LORD."* {Gen. 19:27}

Have a place you can go constantly that has few distractions and is comfortable with good lighting and secluded. Be alone, where it is quiet and you will not be disturbed, where you can pray out loud too.

"Jesus went out as usual to the Mount of Olives, and his disciples followed him." {Luke 22:39}

- Watch your life change as the glory of our Lord Jesus Christ works out in your life.

"If you have any encouragement from being united with Christ, if any comfort from his love, if any fellowship with the Spirit, if any tenderness and compassion, then make my joy complete by being like-minded, having the same love, being one in spirit and purpose. Do nothing out of selfish ambition or vain conceit, but in humility consider others better than yourselves. Each of you should look not only to your own interests, but also to the interests of others. Your attitude should be the same as that of Christ Jesus…" {Philippians 2:1-18}

- Then, Pray, and pray again!

FOURTH: BE OPEN TO THE HOLY SPIRIT

- Unless you are open to Him, how can He teach you?

"I have much more to say to you, more than you can now bear. But when he, the Spirit of truth, comes, he will guide you into all truth. He will not speak on his own; he will speak only what he hears, and he will tell you what is yet to come. He will bring glory to me by taking from what is mine and making it known to you." {John 16:12-14}

- John 1:9: *"The true light that gives light to every one was coming into the world."*

- Do not go into Bible Study with your own agenda; rather let the Holy Spirit direct you.

- Always use discernment and guidance from experienced Bible students!

- Rely on the Power of God!

God's Word is knowable to us! As clear as crystal, in fact more clear than anything ever written in religion or philosophy; clearer than your daily newspaper!

- What clouds it up is when we infuse our own agenda and feeble thinking into it!

REMEMBER TO ALWAYS: BEGIN and END YOUR STUDY IN PRAYER.

- And in the meantime be in prayer. This will take practice and discipline. Do not feel discouraged, it takes time and effort. Be patient and He will come in more power to you!

- You will soon find that prayer will be a second nature to you and will come off with no effort at all! Your instincts will engage in prayer for everything first as you grow and mature in Him!

- Ask the Lord to open your eyes for guidance, insight and application; open your heart to His Will.

"Do your best to present yourself to God as one approved, a workman who does not need to be ashamed and who correctly handles the word of truth." {II Tim 2:15}

CHAPTER IV

"STEP II": "HOW": THE METHOD OF GETTING INTO GOD'S WORD

"My son, if you accept my words and store up my commands within you, turning your ear to wisdom and applying your heart to understanding, and if you call out for insight and cry aloud for understanding, and if you look for it as for silver and search for it as for hidden treasure, then you will understand the fear of the LORD and find the knowledge of God." {Proverbs 2:1-5}

This is the basics on how we can go about studying God's Word. This is called the science of "exegetical method," but there is no need for big words here. These are the basic procedures a pastor or experienced teacher of the Word will learn in Bible School and Seminary to prepare sermons and commentaries, but boiled down in a clearer and simpler way for you to understand and apply.

This will allow you to better understand and apply God's Word and then even teach it to others! These methods are not for the professional Christians only, they are the tools for all disciples of the Lord!

Remember there is no "best way," only that we do it. This study is about placing the "bur" under the saddle to get the hoarse moving, plugging in the computer so we can use it!

A lot of people get lost at first by digging out the family Bible with its beautiful leather cover and thin parchment pages. But find it difficult to understand and then give up because it is a type too hard to read, a font too small for the eyes to track, and a translation that is impossible to follow. Thus make sure you have a good readable translation. There are numerous resources out there, take advantage of them, even Bibles with large easy to read type.

How to Start??? First by:

- Select the verse, book, and passage you wish to study. Either start with Genesis or Matthew, some Bible teachers suggest John. If this is too much, then begin with I Thessalonians, it is easy to understand. The point is to do it. Do not just jump into tough books like Revelation or Romans first. Get to know the Gospels first!

- Discover what our Lord has to say to you! Do not be overwhelmed! Yes the Bible looks ominous and un-climbable, so you just start. Like eating an elephant, you do it by one bite at a time, then one day it will be done!

REMEMBER: It is simply not enough to know what you want to do – You have to know the right way of doing it. Like following a recipe in cooking or working on your car with the manual.

FIRST: PRAY!

- Ask God into your study as your teacher. Ask Him to free your mind from distractions and help you concentrate. You are entering a learning partnership with Christ!

A good plan is essential to any undertaking.

SECOND: LOOK AT THE WHOLE BOOK (i.e. a single book in the Bible) "SEE THE BIG PICTURE"

For example, if you are going to study John, read the book of John in an easy to read translation, like the "New Living Translation." Read it like reading a favorite novel! Enjoy it! Read it through in one setting with no distractions. An average reader will take 30 minutes to 1 hour. That way you will gain an overall understanding. It is best to do this step 2 or 3 times!

- Preview it. Read it like a novel. Try a different translation if you are having difficulty. Then Read slowly and keep re-reading, this will help you remember.

- Like a wide-angle lens – OVERVIEW the big picture. Remember the context! See the whole picture of what is going on. The reason most people do not get it, is because they do not get in it!

- Study whole books; book by book and not just topics or chapters.

- Like putting together a puzzle, start with a corner and then the straight edges. Start with the obvious in its context, and the rest will be revealed from there!

- If you first look too close to a tree, you may not realize you are in a Forrest!

THIRD: READ CAREFULLY. EXAMINE IT WITH A MICROSCOPE.

"WHOLE TO PARTS TO WHOLE"

Start by skimming the whole book, then re-read each chapter at a time more carefully, then reread it very carefully and slowly in a good translation. Then check out other translations, commentaries, and dictionaries. **Repetition is the key to understanding!**

- Read carefully; study it!! Remember most Christians read the Bible, but few will study it! Use the NIV, NKJV, or NASB versions. Do not be distracted and do not stop. Try reading aloud for better concentration.

- Do not read a passage here and there. Read through a whole book through and through systematically, then the chapters, and then study the verses, verse by verse in order. You are not at a buffet.

- Imagine yourself as a participant. As if it is your story. As if you are there.

- Let God speak to you, as the main goal is to know our Lord better, not just to gain more knowledge!

- Look out for topics, logic, and direction.

- Meditate and pray over the passages that "Speak" to you as you re-read, then memorize those key passages.

- Examine what is being said.

I.   First in chapters.
II. Second in Paragraphs
III. Third in Verses.

FOURTH: MAKE USE OF THE BOOK CHART {step VII}.

Write down what God is saying to you and what you have discovered and learned. By doing this, it will allow you to apply it to your life better!

ALWAYS BE AWARE OF THE CONTEXT!!!

- The "nitty-gritty" For REVIEW: read a whole book at least three times in an easy to read translation. Then read each chapter you are studying in a good translation at least three times. Then read the verses, verse by verse in order. Then you will be amazed on how much more you will pick up!

    I.   See it!!!

    II.   Know it!!!

    III.   Do it.!!!

REMEMBER: BIBLE STUDY IS WORK!!!

Growing in the spirit – it is a day by day growth; just like learning to read, the study of mathematics, science, or playing a sport or a musical instrument. It takes time, practice, patience, and effort!

So what about devotional reading?

Can we just read the Bible? After all, the same Spirit that inspired the writers of the Bible can inspire us too? Of course, we also need to read the Bible devotionally regularly as a love letter, for our edification and growth. Devotional reading is one kind of Bible reading that is essential for our growth and discipleship. But devotional reading is not study, and this book is designed to teach you how to study the Bible. And as you learn these principles and tools, your devotional reading will increase in value too because you will be able to instinctually use these common sense tools.

- We must learn to study the Bible to gain more insights into God's character and call for us!

HARD WORK WILL PAY OFF!

CHAPTER V

STEP III: "OBSERVE IT" ASK WHAT DOES IT SAY?!

"Do your best to present yourself to God as one approved, a workman who does not need to be ashamed and who correctly handles the word of truth. Avoid godless chatter, because those who indulge in it will become more and more ungodly." {II TIM 2:15-16}

Now Begin a detailed study of the passage. You thought you already did? Actually you have just begun! This is the step where God's Word becomes clearer and more understandable. This is where you can write down what you see in the chart on "step IV" or in a notebook or diary.

- Effective observation takes time and practice. So be patient.

Observation is taking a careful look of what is going on. And we have to know what is going on before we can act on a plan or action. A good police officer must know the situation before they can intercede correctly: Bible students must know the Word themselves before they can teach it.

Too many people like to dive into a decision without looking at the options and consequences. Too many Bible students will jump into teaching without fully knowing their subject, that is why we have so much bad teaching on TV, and so many false teachings and blatant heresies in the church.

Emotions and desires have been substituted for principle logic and study, greed and power have replaced honoring our Lord!

Like planning a road trip, you need to know where you are going; and then you can look back where you have been: Get Ready to CHART IT! That is to write down what you learn, so you can go back to it and see how you have grown, and to review His incredible Word! This will be step VII.

OBSERVING IS: Before the process of interpretation, asking, "What does it say?" You must do this before you ask what does it mean and how to apply it to your life!

- If you do the opposite as many do, you will **not** go deep enough and allow God's Word to transform you before you respond to that change!

- When we try to do something for God before we are changed is like trying to drive a car manual instead of the car itself: When we are working with the plans only and not the finished product, we will end up accomplishing nothing!

HOW TO DO THE OBSERVATION:

FIRST: Give the Book the "Looks."

- Look for a stated purpose.

- Look for repeated phrases.

- Look for the point.

- Look who is involved?

If you do not know what to "look" for, you will not find much!

- Look for the time of events, the sequence, "once, then, now, will be, etc."

Once you know what to look for, a whole new world opens up to you! You will see the words come to you as marvelous revelations as the Holy Spirit comes upon you!

- Look for persons, places, events, and ideas.

Look for logical Connectives, i.e. Therefore, But, Since, So, Thus, Because, For, That, etc. (Conjunction junction what's your function?) This is very important because it tells us of a transition or summary and application from a logic statement or line of reasoning.

Such as:

- **BUT, Even though, Much More, Yet, Although, Then, and Nevertheless** is a "Contrast," the ideas and information that point to a difference, that set themselves off from each other for comparison and emphasis.

- **As, For, and So,** refer to a "Correlative," that is a mutual dependency, a pair that is closely related to each other.

- **Until, Now, When, Before, After, Since, Where and While** are time or place references and in grammar called "Temporal Connectors." They refer to a time and/or place, use a Bible map to see for yourself.

- **Because, For this reason, For…, and Since** refer to a "Reasoning." They draw conclusions and inferences from the argument and/or information presented. They included causes, motives, justifications, explanations, ideas, acts, sense, and conclusions that result to name a few.

- **Too, Also, As, Just, Likewise, And, So Also, and Like** are "Comparisons." They communicate parallel ideas and facts that are similar or different.

- **So Then, Therefore, As a result, Thus, and Then** are "Results." Usually a consequence, issue or effect that has or will happen. Or a boiling down of the point for an application, the Epistles are filled with them. See a "therefore," then ask what is it there for?

- **That, So That, and In Order That,** are also "results" but with more of a specific Purpose.

- **IF** is a "Condition" flowing from a logical argument, usually starts off with **IF** and concludes a meaning with **THEN**. That the truth depends on the preceding statement or requirement and "If" is the "sound bite" referring to a conclusion that has a condition attached. "Then" is the consequence or conclusion of the argument. "If you touch a hot stove, **then** you will get burned."

Notice other important words!

REMEMBER: VERY EXTREMELY IMPORTANT IS THE CONTEXT!!!

The context is what is going on around the passage you are studying. If you take and read one verse without carefully studying the previous and preceding text, you will miss a great deal and possibly misinterpret what is being said. Some of the preachers on TV love to do this, that is why so many people are being led astray by false teaching!!!

- "Always, always, always beware of the context!!! Cults and false teachers do not do this! So unless you want to start a cult…

THINGS TO OBSERVE:

- Verbs are crucial! If you are not sure of the meaning then check "Webster's." But beware the verb meanings are in English and may not be corresponding to the original meaning {That is why we check several translations, unless you know Greek and Hebrew}. And check **NOUNS** in "Bible Dictionaries!" The context will give you the clues!

- Define the meaning of the important words you are studying, do not assume you know, check it out, by looking them up!

- Look at what is actually being said?

- STUCK? Then try reading aloud!

- Notice the setting.

- Consider words used more than once, and repeated phrases.

- Compare passage/verse too similar verses i.e. "Scripture interprets scripture." Use a "Concordance" or a "Chain Reference Bible."

- Notice the implications

- Notice what is being taught

- Notice the promises

- Notice carefully the underlining principle[s]

- What about the life, work, teaching, presence of Jesus Christ?

- Look out for types of "literary style." That is history, philosophy, drama, poetry, wisdom and law. The Bible is a collection of 66 books written over a 1,500-year period of time, each with its own literary style. Some books are "history" such as I & II Kings and I & II Chronicles. Some books are "Law" such as Leviticus and Deuteronomy. [See appendix A]

- Look at different translations {at least 3, such as NIV, NASB, and a paraphrase like CEV or NLT, or "Amplified Bible"}. Get a "Parallel Bible" it has several translations side by side.

Like looking at a diamond from only one angle is like looking at glass, you see nothing interesting or spectacular. But when you turn the diamond in the light, you see all the facets and depth, so it is with scripture! Looking at various translations side by side is like looking at more facets, it brings out the "3-D" depth, and becomes clearer and easier to understand and then to teach!

Chapter VI

STEP III (B): "OBSERVE IT." ASK WHAT DOES IT MEAN?

"Therefore, my dear friends, as you have always obeyed—not only in my presence, but now much more in my absence—continue to work out your salvation with fear and trembling, for it is God who works in you to will and to act according to his good purpose." {Philippians 2:12-13}

When observing we first ask what it says, then and only then can we observe what it means. Too many people like to get into a hurry and "cut to the chase" for the meaning, and miss out on a lot and even get the meaning wrong! This is the crucial step we have to undertake before we apply it to our lives. There are no easy ways out, or shortcuts to understanding any great works of literature, especially God's Word!

This is the task called "exegesis." This fancy word simply means to study a text carefully, logically and systematically to find the original intended meaning.

This is the process of gaining the "plain truth" of what the passage you are studying means. It is more than just "common sense," and it is common sense. This is where we pick at the text and in so doing we are picking at our hearts and minds!

Remember we must come before the Word with an open heart and mind. This will allow us to discover more of the meaning. We cannot be closed off to His work, and what He has to teach us. We cannot have our own agenda and expectations that takes up all the room in our hearts and minds, that leaves no room for God. We cannot have a mind already made up in our image and limited experience because God is fully capable. But He does not usually steam roll over our will, He allows us to work it out, that is what Philippians 2 is all about.

- If we go to scripture to only be comforted, we will find ourselves spiritually bankrupted.

"I have been crucified with Christ and I no longer live, but Christ lives in me. The life I live in the body, I live by faith in the Son of God, who loved me and gave himself for me." {Gal. 2:20},

We must go before our Lord with the attitude of being poured out before Him with nothing left of our will. Then humbly ask, "please my Lord reveal to me what you want me to learn and to grow. Reveal to me the things you wish me to change, show me how I can be my best for your glory."

- When we go before God with only what we want, all we will hear in return is our echoed assumptions!

"You have seen many things, but have paid no attention; your ears are open, but you hear nothing." {Isaiah 42:20}

We will not gain much with the attitude to just ask God to show us a neat trick, or just help me through this issue, or to just bless me… We must have a lifestyle of conviction and learning. Even when the revelation may shake us out of our tree of comfort. Because everything God has to reveal to us is wonderful. However, we may not see the wonder until years later, or not even until we are called home.

Take comfort that God is sovereign, He is in charge. And He does have a wonderful plan for you. Just beware we cannot go through the committed life of a disciple with the fear of being convicted, or hide in the face of challenge. We cannot tremble as ostriches with our heads in the sand, ignoring the truth that the Holy Spirit has for us. We must be prepared to receive conviction and be willing to change. We need to have an open door to being disturbed. Thus, instead of the "do not disturb" sign on our door to our Lord, it must say, "come on in, disturb all you want." Because God is God and we are not!

- Let God have His way with you!

- We must know our weaknesses and limitations as creatures filled with sin!

- Ask our Lord to open you before Him, to allow yourself to go beyond your culture, education and experience! Then the meaning will come alive!

- We cannot apply what we do not know and understand!

Watch God's Word unfold before you.

These are three crucial areas or rules of "exegesis" that we have to know before we can interpret correctly:

A. **We must be aware of our nature,** that is we, as fallen humans will compare all that we see hear, read and understand to what we have already previously experienced and have learned. We also have to take into account our culture, education, emotional level, and anything else that makes us human and separated from the pure character of God. Thus we are extremely limited in our scope to perceive in a pure logical and precise way {hence why people disagree on every subject known}.

B.   **We must be aware of the nature of Scripture** and the Divine Authors intent. There are several different types of literature or as scholars say "genre" types, by different human writers with different cultures, education and audience, all Divinely inspired.

C.   In the same thought, God has given us a very capable brain and resources to use. In other words "you can do it."

Thus we are the interpreters! What we read filters through our will and perceptions and then we try to make sense of it. It also filters through the types of literature, the "dual nature" of Scripture, which is the Divine Author and the human hand that penned it {God's Word is still infallible and inspired through this dual nature}. We cannot just infuse our experience and limited understanding into the text what is not there and give the credit to the Holy Spirit. We cannot think that our way of thinking is the correct and only way {hence why there are so many denominations}. Because even with the meaning and expression of a word can vary from person to person as we add our perceptions into everything {hence why and how language changes and evolves or de-evolves}.

• The Bible was written by the words of people through their cultures, times and histories, all Divinely inspired by the Holy Spirit!

• The Bible speaks to us through every language and culture that has ever or will ever exist!

When we are aware of this "tension" between the Bibles language, history, literature, and our perceptions, then we can be careful interpreters. We can be on guard, and be in prayer: So that we are focused on Christ and His Word and not ourselves.

See appendix A for list of "genres" literature to be aware of.

Be aware of the CONTEXT!!!!!

There are two main areas of "context" we always need to be aware of and ask the text: "what are the "historical" and what are the "literary "settings?" That is the content of what is going on in the text. What is going on preceding and after our text? The type[s] of literature, and the various cultural factors. What is the point and train of thought? This in scholarly circles is called "Hermeneutics" the study of interpretation. See Appendix A

1. **The Historical Context:** This is the type of literature "genres" that refer to the time period and culture of the people who wrote it and are writing too. The Locations such as the travels of Paul and Jesus, and the time and the sequence of events. This refers to the "occasion" and "purpose" of the Authors intention and how and what it means to them and how and what it means to us.

Such as what is the personal background of Isaiah? What was his position {job}? Who was he writing to? What were the people like {culture and customs}? What were their expectations? These are some of the key questions to ask in order to know what is going on. Carefully reading the text and Bible Encyclopedias, Handbooks, and Dictionaries will give you those insights. But make sure you make your own observations first!

2. The Literary Context: This is the meaning of the words; the Nouns, Verbs, and Adjectives. Both the meaning of the word[s] itself as well as what they mean in their context of sentence structure and surrounding passages. You can do this quite simply by comparing the word you wish to "dig" by looking at a Concordance and at various translations. Such as the word "Denarius" in the Gospels. You may automatically think it is money. And you are right, but what kind of money? What was it used for? What is the amount and its worth? These are critical questions to understand the meaning of the passage. Be aware that the verse numbers paragraphs and chapters are not part of the original text!

When you read, ask, "What does it mean?"

- Look for meanings of words and phrases in the context! Use Bible Dictionaries.

- Look at different translations side by side. I Recommend the N.I.V. or N.A.S.B. for serious study, but the New Living Translation, J.B. Philips, The Message, Amplified, C.E.V., and New Century versions make good insights. Remember they are paraphrases and not accurate translations. Do not take them literally. Just allow them to give you insight. And overview.

- ANALYZE by gathering facts and all the information available to you.

Do not solely rely on commentaries and study Bibles, nothing beats study for yourself, because you will get addicted to rely on them and thus get lazy on your personal studies! Use the commentaries just to see what you may have missed, and what you do not understand!

THINGS TO DO:

- Paraphrase the passage yourself.

- What is supported?

- What are the conclusions?

REMEMBER: Be on the look out for **VERBS**. They are crucial. "Tense, voice, mood, person, & number." You know the stuff from grade school! If you need help check out a grammar textbook, some dictionaries have basic English summaries that will be a great help! Keep in mind the Bible was not written in English! For more serious study check out "Dictionary of New Testament Theology", by Colin-Brown, pub by Regency; which goes through the English words and gives the Greek words and in-depth insights.

The BIG THING TO DO:

Make an emotional identification into the text. Place yourself as a participant, being active in it as if it is your story, as if you are there. We do this naturally when we watch a good movie or TV show. We become a participant vicariously and identify ourselves into it. It captures our attention and interest, as if we are there! Thus, we will cry or laugh, because it touched us. Nothing is more interesting or spectacular than the stories in the Bible. So what is stopping you from being active in it?

THINGS TO VIEW AND ASK AND TO APPLY:

- Ask what is actually being said?

- Try reading aloud!

- Consider nothing insignificant!

- Discuss with other Bible students.

- Have a mentor to ask questions.

- Look for stuff to carry out in your life.

- Write down your questions and what you do not understand. This helps us grow!!!

- What are the implications to be applied?

- What is being taught to be transformed us?

- What are the promises that I can take to heart?

- What about the life, work, teaching, and presence of Jesus Christ? How can I model His Character?

- What is our duty?

- What is God's character?

- Look out for types of "literary style." That is history, philosophy, drama, poetry, wisdom and law. [See appendix A]

- Make a commitment to the meaning.

- Try to write the verse or entire passage in your own words!

- Accept what It says: This is God's Word!

Then, and only after you pursued the questions to your passage, then go to a commentary! There are several good sets available from the classic "Matthew Henry," to more modern versions such as, "With the Word" by Wiersbe and Halley's Bible Handbook." These are single devotional style one volume books, simple to read and understand, and great for general overviews and insights. And there are two great study Bibles I recommend, "NIV Study Bible" or the "New Geneva Study Bible," that have a Bible and notes on most of the passages. Then there are multi-volume sets, pick from such solid Biblical publishers as Tyndale, Inter- Varsity, Zondervan, Moody Press, Eerdmans, Baker, or Thomas Nelson. My personal favorite is, "The Expositor's Bible Commentary", Zondervan, or its condensed version the "NIV Bible Commentary" also by Zondervan.

Ask a pastor you trust because unfortunately there is a lot of garbage out there. Beware and be discerning, always compare Scripture to Scripture, and do not rely just on people's opinions!

- Learning to think "exegetically" will give you a deeper and richer experience in your relationship with Christ because you are in a deeper and richer understanding of His Word!

- Your study and reading will become more enjoyable and exciting!

One of the great themes of the Bible is God's love and saving grace to us who do not deserve it!

Remember Too: Make an emotional identification into the text. Place yourself as a participant, being active in it; As if it is your story; As if you are there!

So why do Christians disagree on a lot of points?

First we may make a lot of "LOGICAL" errors, and misinterpret it and/or take a passage[s] out of its context, or rush through it. We look at one ambiguous text and ignore the clear scores of others. Christians are not perfect and are subject to reasoning and judgment fallacies. Even the greatest scientific minds disagree for these same reasons! Hence why there are so many theories in science, and they are always changing.

Second, we are limited by the education and knowledge we process, and by the information at our disposal, and knowing how to use that information! Our perspectives are limited and we do not always see the big picture, thus our interpretations are sometimes flawed, or the adequate work and effort was not put into it.

Third, One of the biggest causes of errors is our prejudices. That is our preconceived ideas and biases that cloud our thinking. Such as believing in a particular mode of baptism or end time theory. We may grow up in a church that practices "believers baptism" or "infant baptism" only, thus are unwilling to look deeper theologically at the other views.

People tend to rationalize their faulty beliefs instead of researching and discovering the facts for themselves. Or they do not want to know or grow beyond their limited experience, or base decisions on emotions and do not seriously see the logic.

Fourth, we are still full of sin and fall way short, thus we are susceptible to the influences of Satan and are unable to reason with true perfection!

For example in John 1:1 the Jehovah's Witnesses believe Jesus is not God, but "a god" as Lucifer to is a god in their theology. In I Corinthians 15:29, the Mormons believe it is OK to baptize people who have already died. In Mark 16:18, some American Appalachian sects handle poisonous snakes to prove their faith. Some Bible teachers on TV use 3 John 2 as an excuse to teach the "health and wealth" gospel. Yet when you examine these texts they do not teach any of those things! These are classic cases of bad interpretation for the reasons fore mentioned.

- The Bible does not teach anything we please.

- The Bible cannot mean something else from what it does say. The Bible cannot mean what it never meant!

What about studying topics? If you want to study a topic in the Bible the Concordance is your main resource. By looking up the subject and then studying the various passages on the subject, and in their context. Also be on the lookout for words of similar meaning. Such as studying "gossip," you need to also look up "tongue."

The "Chain-Reference Bible" and the "The New Treasury of Scripture Knowledge" by Nelson will be indispensable. Other resources are "Naves Topical Bible" and "Meredith's Book of Bible Lists" by Bethany: These are wonderfully helpful works!

- You will follow the same steps as studying a Book, but also comparing passages side by side. Newer computer software from "Nelson," Parson's," and "Zondervan" make this job a synch!

- Make sure you read and study all the passages in the Bible on your subject. If you do not, you will make a lot of "Exegetical Fallacies," that is a lot of misunderstandings and mistakes. Not studying all the passages is the favorite method of some Bible teachers today who carelessly string a set of verses out of their context and place together and thus lead their flocks astray! "Haste makes waste!"

- Make sure you have the correct meaning, double check with good commentaries.

- Be on the lookout for the context!

- Do not be too dependent on topics, nothing beats the study of a Book in the Bible for a well-rounded disciple grounded in the Lord!

"Knock, and the door will be open for you" Matt 7:7

We learn by doing. So, do it!

CHAPTER VII

STEP IV: "QUESTIONS": ASK AND LEARN!!!

"Command and teach these things. Don't let anyone look down on you because you are young, but set an example for the believers in speech, in life, in love, in faith and in purity. Until I come, devote yourself to the public reading of Scripture, to preaching and to teaching. Do not neglect your gift, which was given you through a prophetic message when the body of elders laid their hands on you. Be diligent in these matters; give yourself wholly to them, so that everyone may see your progress. Watch your life and doctrine closely. Persevere in them, because if you do, you will save both yourself and your hearer." {I Tim. 4:11-16}

Asking questions are the tools to take God's Word and examine it. After this, we learn and grow. Just as a child will learn, so must we for we are God's children. This is the step that goes along side of IIIB and turbo charges it. It causes us to think deeper and gather the additional information we need to be challenged and then to grow.

- When we are challenged to grow we become better disciples for His kingdom!

Like looking at a great work of art, most people who pass it by and make a sly comment, while another person will see the greatness and rave about it. The difference is some people know what to look for. Do you? The same is with the Bible. You will not find much unless you know how to look.

Remember: Effort is essential. You need to put in "Bible Elbow Grease" and the rewards are plentiful. Knowledge is power… God's power for you!

To play baseball, you need a bat. Asking questions is our bat to know God's Word.

THE TOOL BOX TO GOD'S WORD:

THE SIX BIG Q'S WE MUST ALWAYS ASK!

1. WHO: Who are the people? Who did it? Who can do it? Who is it talking about?

2. WHAT: What is it saying? What is it talking about? What is happening? What did they do?

3. WHERE: Where are they going? Where did it happen? Where will it take place?

4. WHEN: When did it happen? When will it happen? When can it happen?

5. HOW: How did it happen? How can it happen? How was something done?

6. WHY: Why did he say that? Why did he do that? Why did they go there?

ASK WHICH ONE OR MORE OF THESE APPLIES.

Note, not all the questions and "STEPS" will apply to every verse. Use discernment and common sense that is good judgment!

MORE TOOLS: GOD'S WORD IS A PLUMBERS PLUNGER TO THE WORLD'S LEAKING TOILET!

ASK THESE ADDITIONAL QUESTIONS:

1. Are there any commands?

2. Are there any contrasts?

3. Are there things repeated?

4. Is there cause and effect?

5. Is there a problem and solution?

6. Are there any promises?

7. Are there any connections to other parts of the Bible?

8. Notice the setting! You may need to check a Commentary or Bible Encyclopedia on this for some books. For example, in Philippians Paul speaks of being "joyful" and "trust in the Lord," and "be anxious for nothing." At first glance, no big deal just what you may expect to find in the Bible. But careful study and investigation will reveal that

Paul was writing in prison tied to the dirt floor laying in his own "excrement's," eating what was thrown to him on the dirt and waiting for his execution! Thus a new and deeper meaning comes to us, so we can trust Christ in all the situations we could ever face!

9. Compare your verse with other similar verses. Some Bibles have a list of verses on the margin or in the middle of the columns, which is what they are for. If you do not have one, pick up a "Chain-Reference Bible" or get "The New Treasury of Scripture Knowledge" by Nelson. These are wonderfully helpful works!

Use your imagination! Let the Bible come alive in you!!!

ONCE YOU KNOW THESE QUESTIONS THEY WILL BE AUTOMATIC:

I.E. How hard is Who, What Where, When, How, and Why? You should remember them from the third grade.

Check out Appendix C for a list of resources and how to use them.

Chapter VIII

STEP V: "KNOW IT"!!!

"Now the Bereans were of more noble character than the Thessalonians, for they received the message with great eagerness and examined the Scriptures every day to see if what Paul said was true." {Acts 17:11}

Just as the Customs Officer asks you with a deep stern and convicting look when you enter a country, "do you have anything to declare," so must we declare Christ with even more passion and conviction! And we can only do it with knowing it, knowing Him and His Word.

This is the step that helps us "internalize" what we are learning. This is the process of interpretation, which is determining the meaning of the text. Not just what it says, but what we do with it. Thus when we ask what does it mean, we then need to determine how it's going to "fit into" our life.

You can easily know something without it ever effecting you. Such as watching a tragedy on the news, but never giving it a second thought. We must never allow God's Word to be in that category!!!

It is one thing to believe in the existence of cars, another thing to learn how to drive them. Step IV helps us to know about the existence of cars, or "God's decrees." Step V shows us that we need to take ownership of it, and we must do this before we can drive it. Thus the knowing and internalizing comes before the application. We have to be in tune with what and why we do something before we can do it effectively and grow from it.

It is like a circle, knowing it must precede doing, yet doing can open the door to knowing. And then the knowing will increase the doing…

"It is not enough to just know it. It must be rooted in our very hearts, minds and soul!"

We must ask ourselves, "How can the teaching about God's Word relate to my problems, feelings, values, attitudes, situations, ambitions, needs, desires, and relationships."

START LOOKING FOR THE ANSWERS:
"Interpretation" is the process of determining the meaning of the text.

You can not make an application until you are a "new life," that is we must be the people of God to be able to do the work of God!

WHAT YOU WANT TO DO IS:

• Discover and understand what the divine author means.

Example: When Jesus says He is the bread of life, does this mean He is the loaf of bread?

WHAT DOES SOMETHING MEAN AND WHY IS IT THERE?

• Discover the historical and cultural background.

• Be sure your information is correct!!!

- Use good commentaries, Study Bibles, and Bible dictionaries.

Digging Personally:

- How are you encouraged and strengthened?

- Where have you fallen short, and how can you improve?

- What do you now intend to do with the information given to you by the Holy Spirit through God's Word?

Remember: *"All scripture is inspired by God and profitable for teaching..."* We must never substitute doctrine for personal beliefs! (II Timothy 3:16).

Observation makes interpretation easy.

Be Aware of Context!!!

Like cutting a beautiful flower and studying it as if it were a whole plant and ignoring the stems, roots and leaves. The flower will wither and die without the nourishment from the rest of the plant. So it is when we take a verse out of its context!

Study the verses better and slowly. Are you taking something out of its context? The chapter and verses **are not inspired**. The publisher to make reading easier has added them in.

Be aware:

You will get into big trouble if you try to read into the text what is not there! A lot of pastors today like to find "secret meanings" from the text. Thus, books like the "Bible Code" become popular. But there is no code other than the one made up by its authors by backward engineering a formula into the text. And their formula does not work nor does it have any consistency.

- THERE ARE NO SECRET MEANINGS {except some apoplectic writings, but they are not a "secret" just temporally hidden, they will be plainly revealed in time}!!!!

- You are not to dig out what is not there, you are not to send your "ferret" {a rodent that likes to hunt for things, similar to a mink} mind to bring back what is not there. Can I be any clearer?

Look at the ADJECTIVES:

My mother is in the catering business, and when I look at her gourmet cooking magazines, I notice all kinds of adjectives such as "Perfect, The Best, Favorite, Fine, Blissful, Great, Superb, Fantastic, Incredible, and Pleasingly" and I could go on and on! The writers use these adjectives to describe and express the enthusiasm that they are experiencing. This excitement comes manly form the tastes and pleasures they received from the quality of the food. From the way it is prepared to the way it is presented to them. All centering on the work, experience, effort and quality of ingredients put into it by the chef.

When we are reading God's Word we are a chef preparing a marvelous and fantastic feast, what we get out of it will be what we put into it, from the quality of the ingredients to the time it takes to cook will determine how transformed you will be!

To receive any true benefit from scripture, we have to be in it deeply and earnestly, plunging ourselves into the depths of the words and details. To be identified in the Word of God, experiencing it for ourselves.

To receive our profit from our investment, we must seize the adjectives with enthusiasm and vigor, like partaking in your favorite meal, from its aroma to its taste and consumption!

Taking the aroma of the words and keep at it until the taste and meaning are enveloping and transforming your life!

- Getting into God's Word must affect our every day life. How we think, how we feel; this is where our values come from.

- We are to be active in God's Word even when we are not reading it.

- A life based analysis, synthesis, valuing, organizing, and comprehending our Lord Jesus Christ.

- To our very "existential core" that is the soul and being of who we are to Christ!

- We must have the confidence that the Bible is truth, and the truth is living within us. Without such confidence, we can no way be transformed ourselves, let alone infect others with the Gospel message! This is knowing It!

- WE must allow God's Word to bend and break our will and desires over to His!

What did God say to you today?

Is there a sin in your life that needs to be confessed and repented?

What did God nourish you with today?

Are you appreciating it?

- Are you not only receiving the great benefits, but practicing them to others around you?

- Are you a changed person as a result of receiving the Word?

Service is who we are in Christ, and not so much what we do for Christ!

Do not skip your meals in God's Word!

CHAPTER **IX**

STEP VI: "APPLICATION"!!!

"Therefore, I urge you, brothers, in view of God's mercy, to offer your bodies as living sacrifices, holy and pleasing to God—this is your spiritual act of worship. Do not conform any longer to the pattern of this world, but be transformed by the renewing of your mind. Then you will be able to test and approve what God's will is—his good, pleasing and perfect will. For by the grace given me I say to every one of you: Do not think of yourself more highly than you ought, but rather think of yourself with sober judgment, in accordance with the measure of faith God has given you." {Rom. 12:1-3}

Just Do It!!! And away we go!!

This is the step where the rubber of the tires meets the road. All the previous five steps lead up to this. This is the main point of why we study the Bible, to do something with it. Of course we all do something with it, either we ignore it or we are transformed by it.

We can master all the previous steps, even be transformed by the Word; but, if nothing comes from it, it is meaningless and nearly worthless. This is one of the main points of the book of James. Our faith must have a response to it. Yes we may be saved, but what good is it if we do noting with it. With the knowledge we have learned, then it becomes our responsibility! And then we are to ask, "how then do I live?" What can I do now, today, or this week to implement the instructions given to me with my relationship to Christ, to others, and to myself?

True application comes only from the result of a life transformed. You may do good works without Christ, but they are out of a sense of obligation and guilt, and not out of a response to our sin nature that has been covered by grace creating a willing and loving heart to model the character of our Lord!

- The fruits of the Spirit are the result of a life transformed by Christ.

How we are un-transformed: *"The acts of the sinful nature are obvious: sexual immorality, impurity and debauchery; idolatry and witchcraft; hatred, discord, jealousy, fits of rage, selfish ambition, dissensions, factions and envy; drunkenness, orgies, and the like. I warn you, as I did before, that those who live like this will not inherit the kingdom of God."* {Gal. 5:19-21}

How we are transformed: *"But the fruit of the Spirit is love, joy, peace, patience, kindness, goodness, faithfulness, gentleness and self-control. Against such things there is no law. Those who belong to Christ Jesus have crucified the sinful nature with its passions and desires. Since we live by the Spirit, let us keep in step with the Spirit. Let us not become conceited, provoking and envying each other."* {Gal 5:22-26}

- God uses His Word to transform us, it is what we do, and what He does. He sends us His Spirit, we respond.

REMEMBER: Application comes out of a Changed life. And leads to a life transformed!

Jesus urged us to build our lives on His Word.

"*For false Christs and false prophets will appear and perform great signs and miracles to deceive even the elect—if that were possible. See, I have told you ahead of time. "So if anyone tells you, There he is, out in the desert, do not go out; or, Here he is, in the inner rooms, do not believe it. For as lightning that comes from the east is visible even in the west, so will be the coming of the Son of Man."* {Matthew 7:24-27}

- What must I do to make God's Word real in me?

- When will what I learned end up in my day planner?

- What is my response?

- The Word of God is to lead us to model the character of Christ, to be formed in the image of God.

Do Not Forget Bible Verse Memorization!!!

Mediate over the passage you are studying, that is reflect on it, ponder it, think of it so that you are seriously going over the passage over and over in your mind. Then the memorization will become easier since the verse[s] have rooted in you!

Then the life transformed will take effect much easier and completely!

- Discipleship is following Christ and not just beliefs, ideas, or causes. Too many people are devoted to a doctrine or a cause in the name of Christ, but not Christ Himself! That is how we got the Inquisition and Crusades.

Big Tip Read Your Bible and verses you wish to memorize into a Tape Player. You can do this with NOTES, TEXT, READINGS, and etc. Then, play it back while driving, or at the mall, or anywhere, with a "Walk-Man." You can do this with any of your notes, study material, information you have to memorize, even terms and words for science or a foreign language, or math formulas. This is one of the best ways to study!!!!!!!!!!!!! THIS WORKS!!!!!!!!!!!

ASK YOURSELF THESE FIVE QUESTIONS:

1. What illustration or analogy can I develop to remember the truth it contains, stories tell?

2. How does the truth apply to my life?

3. What is my personal prayer regarding these truths? Write it out and present it to the Lord.

4. What changes/improvements could I make in light of the truth? List several.

5. How should I carry out these changes?

SOMETHING TO CONSIDER:

- Satan would like nothing better than for you not to do the above!!! Do not procrastinate. Press on!!! Do not assume that because you understand something that you have applied it!!! Do not get frustrated. You cannot expect instant results.

- Studying the Word without putting any application to it is like buying a nice new car, taking it home and keeping it in your garage. Then all you do is sit in it and pretend you are driving, listening to the radio, but never actually turning it on and going anywhere with it.

• When we read God's Word and do nothing with it, we become the biggest fools in the universe!

This area of putting feet to God's Word is the most neglected aspect of our Christian life! But it is at this part where our lives change and God uses us to change others.

"For this reason I remind you to fan into flame the gift of God, which is in you through the laying on of my hands. For God did not give us a spirit of timidity, but a spirit of power, of love and of self-discipline. So do not be ashamed to testify about our Lord, or ashamed of me his prisoner. But join with me in suffering for the gospel, by the power of God, who has saved us and called us to a holy life—not because of anything we have done but because of his own purpose and grace. This grace was given us in Christ Jesus before the beginning of time."
{I Tim. 1:6-9 NIV}

If no application comes to your mind, pray, and pray again. Let God show you His way, not our way.

- Pray to ask God how to implement His truth to you.

- Tell Others. Remember Matthew 28. The best way to remember what you learn is to teach others.

- Accountability. Let someone else you know and trust hold you to your promises especially as it relates to the study of God's Word.

Beware!! The more knowledge we have, the more accountability and responsibility we have to God. This is why Moses was not allowed into the Promised Land, when he seemingly disobeyed God by hitting a rock with his staff. It may not seem much of an offense to us, but before God Moses knew better then anyone else. Fortunately for us today we have grace!

"But it has now been revealed through the appearing of our Savior, Christ Jesus, who has destroyed death and has brought life and immortality to light through the gospel. And of this gospel I was appointed a herald and an apostle and a teacher. That is why I am suffering as I am. Yet I am not ashamed, because I know whom I have believed, and am convinced that he is able to guard what I have entrusted to him for that day. What you heard from me, keep as the pattern of sound teaching, with faith and love in Christ Jesus. Guard the good deposit that was entrusted to you— guard it with the help of the Holy Spirit who lives in us."
{II Tim. 1:10-14}

- You can stand in an ice-cream shop all day long and stare at all of the flavors, but no enjoyment or satisfaction will come until you bite into a scoop for yourself!

Remember the Word of God's purpose is to transform us into the image of God, to model His character!

Chapter X

STEP VII: "CHARTING YOUR PATH"

"Then Jesus said to his disciples, "If anyone would come after me, he must deny himself and take up his cross and follow me. For whoever wants to save his life will lose it, but whoever loses his life for me will find it. What good will it be for a man if he gains the whole world, yet forfeits his soul? Or what can a man give in exchange for his soul?"
{Matt. 16:24-26}

This is the step where you keep track of what you learn. Pastors get better at preaching and teaching not just by practice and study, but also by going over what they taught in the past. Playing their tapes and re-reading and reviewing their studies. They can see where they have been to go further ahead. It also acts as an archive of learning, a database of what we have learned that we can draw from.

By writing it down in an organized fashion, God's Word will become more clear and crisp. We are able to record what God says to us, this way we will be able to take more ownership and then greater transformation. We will be able to look back and see and remember what we have discovered, so it will make us better disciples and children of God, and teachers of the Word and will show you how to apply the principles to your life and others! And of course, you will be able to remember more!

We then can look back and see God at work in our lives and will be a great encouragement in times of struggle, and in times of joy. You can review a passage you did in the past and see how you have learned and grew, and quickly brush up on passages that you are being taught from others.

A BOOK CHART WILL HELP YOU GREATLY

- This is where you write down what you learn from the previous steps.

- It will allow you to see a whole book at a glance.

- It will allow you to reach and remember what you learn much, much faster and better.

- It will reveal the theme of a chapter paragraph just at a glance.

THIS CHART IS IN FOUR (4) SECTIONS

1ST: "Chapter and Paragraph titles."
This is where you can summarize chapters and whole books in your own words or paraphrase a verse[s]. You can create an outline of the passage by making your own titles for paragraphs and insights. STEPS I and II come into play here!

- Develop your own chapter and paragraph titles.
- Be creative. Try harder.
- Be sure it describes the passage and relates to it!
- Do not be too general.
- Keep them short so they are easy to remember.

Use your individual unique way of expressing yourself.

2nd: "OBSERVATION: What does it say?"
This is where you use STEP III, and write your observations.

- Bible Statements.
- Give the "looks"
- Observe grammar & literary style

3rd: "OBSERVATION: What does it mean?"
This is where you use STEPS IIIB & IV.

- Ask what are the implications.
- Ask your questions here!
- Who, What, Where, When, How, and Why.

4th: "APPLICATION: How does it apply to my life?"
This is where we use Steps V & VI.

- How does it apply to my life?
- How can I implement God's Word into my life?
- What will I do with this information?
- **When will I do it?**

"OTHER INFORMATION" This is where you can write down your prayers and doodles.

WHEN YOU READ THE BIBLE: Remember to Pray!!!

- Pray, pray, pray! Be continuously in prayer as you read His Word.
- Ask questions.

- Use all the previous six- (6) steps when applicable.
- Then write it down. Do not want to use this book chart, then keep a diary or notebook.

Don't' hesitate to record other useful information, especially your prayers!!

REMEMBER:

- Study the chapters and paragraphs first!!!

- Then write your outline, you can do this by assigning names for the paragraphs. Use steps I through VI.

THE CHART *"For the word of God is living and active. Sharper than any double-edged sword, it penetrates even to dividing soul and spirit, joints and marrow; it judges the thoughts and attitudes of the heart"*

STEP I & II: PRAY & HOW	STEP III: OBSERVE IT	STEP IIIB & IV: QUESTIONS	STEP V & VI: KNOW IT & Apply
<u>Scripture:</u> Chapter and Paragraph Titles? PRAY, direct your will, make a commitment ; Look at the whole book, then Chapters, & then verses	<u>Observations:</u> What Does it Say? Give the "looks'" observe grammar & literary style	<u>Observations:</u> What Does it mean? Ask questions, be aware of making errors, use "tools," implications, " who what where, when, how, & why"	*<u>Application:</u> How Does It Apply to Me? Make an emotional identification! Look for the answers, dig personally, let it effect you!*
Passage:_____			
Key Verse{s}:	Biblical Statements:	My Questions:	What Will I Do:
Key Word{s}:			When Will I Do It? BE OBEDIENT!!!

OTHER INFORMATION AND PRAYER ITEMS:

THE CHART A *"For the word of God is living and active. Sharper than any double-edged sword, it penetrates even..."*

STEP I & II: PRAY & HOW	STEP III: OBSERVE IT
<u>Scripture:</u> Chapter and Paragraph Titles? PRAY, direct your will, make a commitment Look at the whole book, then Chapters, & then verses	<u>Observations:</u> What Does it Say? Give the "looks'" observe grammar & literary style
Passage:_____ Key Verse{s}: Key Word{s}:	 Biblical Statements:

OTHER INFORMATION AND PRAYER ITEMS:

THE CHART B "...to dividing soul and spirit, joints and marrow; it judges the thoughts and attitudes of the heart"

STEP IIIB & IV: QUESTIONS	STEP V & VI: KNOW IT & Apply
Observations: What Does it mean? Ask questions, be aware of making errors, use "tools," implications, " who what where, when, how, & why"	**Application:** How Does It Apply to Me? Make an emotional identification! Look for the answers, dig personally, and let it effect you!
My Questions:	What Will I Do: When Will I Do It? BE OBEDIENT!!!

I hear and forget. I see and I remember. I do and I understand."

Part II

INTO THY WORD LEADERS GUIDE FOR GROUP STUDY

This is designed for the small group or retreat or group study to go through to better understand how to dig into God's Word. This is a "curriculum" that can be used to further challenge you individually as well.

Introduction:

This is a simple easy to learn and teach curriculum on how we can study and know God's Word. It is designed and has been used for High School and Adult groups very successfully! It requires little effort on the leaders part, other than to read through it, and have a love and desire to get into God's Word yourself. Because if you do not have a love and passion to be intimate with God, then how will you be able to communicate it to those God has entrusted to you for discipleship?

The opportunity is yours to put more into it if you have the time. If you are in a pinch all you need to do is read through it first and go for it, the Lord will use you! But as with anything important, the more effort the "more" of results you will receive in your own life and then impart on your students.

So the hard part is the maturity of the leader, the easy part is teaching the subject. So spend time in prayer for the Lord to use you, for Him to guide you, read through the material and go for it in love and grace, because He loves you and will use you!

Remember we can not do the work of God unless we are the People of God, we cannot teach what we do not do!

The Format:

The student workbook is laid out for you to study on your own individually {which I strongly recommend before teaching it}, or to use it in large groups, and small groups. It is very flexible. It is designed for high school through young adults, but many older adult groups will benefit from it too. You can customize it for most any situation: For youth groups, small groups, Sunday school, retreats, or personal study. The student workbook is the "how too" into God's Word. It contains the essential elements written in an outline format, with ample scripture references. It is designed for the student to go through it alone or in a group. You can give it to your students in advance, maybe two weeks so they can read through and familiarize themselves with it, or you can just jump in. "It is user friendly."

THERE ARE THREE MAIN SECTIONS TO THIS STUDY:

1. Sessions I through VI "The why and importance of the Bible."

You can cut this part down. Some teachers will only do half of this first section for time constraints. But if it is for a lack of interest, you have a problem. I feel this would be unfortunate because many young people today hunger for spirituality but cannot find it anywhere. They may have been in churches or families that in the name of Christ have been abused by them. Or have been influenced by the secular mindset, or just do not want to give up their rights to themselves.

But if we do not have a love for what we are doing and a strong reason and purpose, we will soon leave it behind. Let us not leave God's Word behind!

2. Sessions VII through XIV Is the "How to read the Bible."

This Is based on the "Into Thy Word Steps" what I will call the "Workbook," which is the "how" to exegete and know Scripture. For these lessons you can use a computer software program and print off a chapter of Scripture in different translations such as the NIV, KJV, NASB, and various paraphrases. Romans 12 is a good one to start with, lots of stuff to dig into. Or you can dig into a smaller Book, such as II, III John, Jude or…it's up to you.

3. Session XV is the "Chart"

This is the "How" to put into practice all the steps. This can be one lesson, as an overview, or you can use it to go through a book of the Bible, or if you are ambitious the whole Bible {may take you 10 years}. Make copies of the Chart for each student, have a supply of Bibles and resource books, see Appendix C.

The leaders guide:

The leaders guide is divided into 7 sections for each lesson.

First is the Bible study "Leaders Study" for the leaders to work through issues essential for leading this study and for personal discipleship and edification. Thus the thrust of the leader's study is to prepare yourself to teach, and to reach the people the Lord has sent to you. We have to be the people of God in order to do the work of God.

Second is the outline of the lesson with approximate times. Now each group is different, as some love to talk and discuss and others will sit there like cows staring at you. Remember there are more questions and activities than the normal time of a class will allow, so plan accordingly. Perhaps as you go over the material, mark the parts your students need to know and make sure you have time to cover them. Save the rest for when you have time, or go back to it after a year or so as review.

Third: This is the opening option where a story or activity designed to start off the subject for that day and set the tone. Give them something to start their leaning process, leading to how they will know it and then apply it to their lives. You may not need to do this section with some older adult groups, because they may just want to jump right in. Find out from your group how they would like to proceed. For additional story helps, get the

Books, "Hot Illustrations for Youth Talks" by Youth Specialties. There are 3 volumes, or go to the web site "Youthpastor.com."

Fourth: Is the "curriculum" in the student workbook. You can use this as your "talk," or you can have people read it in advance {good luck with short attention span teens!}, or you can read it in the class, or have students read it {give it to them a week in advance, this works great with teens}. I have found it best for the teacher to read it, and give sections to your students to read. It all depends on your group. Steps VII to XV can be a group effort, as you can combine the talk and discussion together. Because you will actually be studying and digging into a text, thus learn as you do as you teach.

It is a good idea to give the scriptures to various students in advance to read aloud when called on. Make sure they are comfortable to read in public and they are not wasting class time looking up the passages. Have them booked marked and ready. {Of course looking up passages is never a waist of time, it is more of time management. Five (5)minutes spent looking up passages is five (5) minutes taken away from discussion and application.}

This takes the "teacher show" approach away and gives more of the learning over to the students themselves. Power point works wonders with this or any study, just type in the key pints {bullets} and click away as you give the lesson.

Fifth: Is the discussion questions. They are designed to be done in a small group setting, but again can be used individually or in a large group. I recommend you break into groups of 4 to 6, you do not need adults if you are teaching high school students as long as you come back for questions and answers. They are capable to lead themselves with guidance and support. There are specific questions to ask your students to spur discussion, and to get them thinking and challenge them into the Lord's service. {Service is an outgrowth of discipleship, a response of gratitude to the grace we have been given that covered our guilt and fallen separated nature. God's Word will challenge and lead people to the Lord's path, it will convert, convict and teach. The only thing to worry about is not to get in the way of God.} The discussion for the first several sections are questions in 4 parts:

First is an "opener" to spur thinking and get people talking.

Second is a "to know it" where we are going over the essential information we are learning.

Third is "getting deeper" by changing the way we think from our way to God's way, thus taking ownership of what is being taught.

Fourth is the "application", sometimes a homework assignment, or something to ponder {thinking deeper}.

The rest of the sessions are designed as an adventure to dig into the "steps," learning by doing!

These questions can be tailored to age and time constraints, along with sections to go deeper in their spiritual life. You can put them in your own words. Later on, there will be charts to incorporate what was learned, and to use in their personal devotions and study. Encourage students to make use of them, and not throw them out, as they progress they can see it as a journal on their spiritual walk.

Sixth: This is the "Going Deep" section and it can be used in the small group or back in the large group after the Q&A. They are "Spiritual exercises" to help us to engage and deepen the classic Christian disciplines of silence, solitude, study, prayer, worship, sacrifice and celebration. I suggest that you bring them back as a large group for this section until they feel comfortable in the small groups. Staying in a large group will bring your group deeper in their collective spiritual life, and more community and depth to your group dynamics. Keep in mind this may not work with some people {especially multigenerational Christians in a constrained church}. They may feel uncomfortable. Just reassure and encourage them, and when they are ready, try it again. Some people are just not ready for deep spiritual stuff.

You can find other examples of contemplative Christian exercises such as the "Jesus Prayer," "Lectio Divina," the "Ignatian Awareness Examen" and other classic forms of prayerful attention. Most of these are, or have been practiced in Monasticism {monks and nuns}, and were "the baby that was thrown out with the bath" by the reformation. Calvin and Luther both practiced these all of their reformed lives, and Calvin wrote extensively on their benefit!

You may find these recourses in a Catholic bookstore. The ones in this series were designed by me over the years and are not from catholic resources.

In a contemplative approach to youth and adult ministry, churches engage in exercises that help them become more aware and attentive to God's presence and call in their lives.

Going deeper requires "baby steps," that is you may not be able to do this section all at once. You may start off with some of the aspects in this leader's guide depending on the spiritual maturity of the leader and the students. Not behavior maturity, although this is important, but rather spiritual maturity, the depth that we have gone in our personal walk with prayer, study of His Word, and devotions.

I strongly suggest that the leader experience and work through these issues first before challenging their group with them. You cannot lead where you have not been!

As a result of using classic devotions, most churches report a "spiritual awakening" among young people in their congregations!

As one 15-year-old states, "*I feel a greater sense of God's presence in my life … a warm flame has become ignited that was not there before.*"

If you are not going to be using the "going deep," then remember to pray as you normally do, and try to incorporate the "going deep" gradually. You can repeat them from various sections, or use them as they are. These lessons are designed to take students into a deeper ownership of their spiritual journey, and a deeper commitment to what is being taught and learned. This is what Christ called us to do, to make disciples, and grow closer to Him. We cannot just rely on our beliefs and actions because we have to be a changed person before we can model changes to ourselves and then others!

Seventh: "The Close:" This is the last section after the small groups where you can do the "going deep," close in a song, or in prayer, or both. You can have a question and answer time {this I strongly recommend} to go over what is being missed in some of the discussion groups. You can go over the main points of the lesson, or share what you are learning and growing in. I have found it best to have a quick question and answer session first then do the "Going Deep." And if you do not know the answer, it's okay. Just find out from your pastor, apologetical book, or Internet source and get back to them by the following meeting. Then go over and remind them of the application challenge, close with the "Going Deep" and then in prayer. There is no set way or right way, it is up to you, what your group needs, and their maturity level. Just remember the importance of prayer.

So How Do I Start?

First read through the student's workbook {the first part of this book}, then the leaders guide section by section as you get ready to teach it. It is best to at least skim the whole thing too, to give you a general overview. After you have gone over it, highlight the sections and options you will do, and go over in the "lesson" section and pick the points you wish to cover. You may not have enough time to cover it all. You can make it into a talk, re-say it in your own words, just read it with interest and excitement, let them read it themselves, or read it like "Jeopardy" questions. Be creative! Do not spend too much of the class time with this, even though it is the most important part of the lesson. Encourage the students to read the section in advance before the class.

Do not be overwhelmed, this is a 15-week curriculum {which can be extended, especially if you go through a whole epistle after completing the 15-week sessions}, so go step by step. You should at least be going over the section you are teaching first before you teach. And you should have read the entire workbook before you start this series, so you know were you are going. You do not need to know every detail ahead, just the general theme, as you get close to each new section, then re-read it and you will pick it up fast. Each section builds on the previous section. {If you are worried that if a student misses a session they will be lost. They could be, but encourage them to spend 15 minutes reading through the student workbook what they have missed, and they will be fully caught up!}

You may spend a couple of hours doing this whole overview before you begin to teach this series. Then before each meeting spend as much time as you can in prayer, and at least 20 minutes reading over the section. You will find it will almost teach itself! But as with anything, the more prepared you are the better the outcome will be.

The format is up to you and your teaching style. You can just have a discussion with the workbook by having everyone read a chapter before they come, use this curriculum as is, or customize it. If you are new to teaching, I suggest you follow it. This series has more questions and options than normal time constraints will allow. The reason is simple, sometimes groups will not engage in discussion, the extra material is to prevent dead air. Or, sometimes the students want more, so you can give it to them to take home. Every group is different. Sometimes special resources are suggested that you do not have time to get or forgot, that is why we have several options! Or if they skipped a week, all the pertinent information is in the student workbook.

You may want to extend the number of meetings for a deeper walk into His Word. Or you can mark off what you did go over, and a year latter come back to this series and cover what you did not do before with a general introduction, and go through a book of the Bible. This reinforces the importance of this study and gives time for their minds to develop and practice what they have learned. So when you come back to it, more discussion should develop, as their experience has increased.

To be a successful leader and discipler, we have to dispel the myth of trying to be popular or eloquent. We need to be real, to do our best, and have a passion and love for what we are teaching and to those who we are teaching. And to begin we need to know what maturity is all about, because if we do not get this important facet, all we try to model and teach will unravel and be meaningless to those we are trying to teach.

SESSION I

"The Importance of God's Word"

Leaders Study: "Maturity"

"Therefore we do not lose heart. Though outwardly we are wasting away, yet inwardly we are being renewed day by day. For our light and momentary troubles are achieving for us an eternal glory that far outweighs them all. So we fix our eyes not on what is seen, but on what is unseen. For what is seen is temporary, but what is unseen is eternal." {II Corinthians 4:16-18}

We must realize that our Lord can and will bring goodness and glory to any situation that He is glorified. That is even through our weakness and failures, through our letdowns and discouragements, Christ is there loving us and encouraging us. Paul knew this first hand and lived it out in his life and ministry, as must we. Whatever our circumstance, we need to see that it impales in significance to the eternity we have to come. This world and life is a dress rehearsal, and a mere shadow to what is to come. So keep the focus on what is ahead that is Christ our Lord. Because we will enjoy our Lord for all time, so let us live for eternity and not just today. We may not see the truths of eternity in our present condition, so let us press on to the goal anyway, and then at the end we will see what was life is all about.

One of the clearest evidences of being a mature Christian is an increased awareness and knowledge for the need to be in Christ, and not to be to ourselves. When we have an increased need that goes beyond ourselves, an increasing need that goes beyond our self-confidence, then we are becoming mature. This means we are to be in on our Lord and the Holy Spirit as our focus. Then, our self-confidence becomes rooted and dependent in Christ working through us. So we are not to be self-driven but Christ driven. Thus resulting in our will to be in total surrender to God's {Gal 2} will as the driving force for our existence. So Christ is first in our life and not our selfish will and desires.

Too many people feel they are too busy to contemplate their existence, just ask anyone and you will be surprised on the answers. Yet God created us for a purpose, but most give little to no credence to it, even Christians do not think about their purpose and call. We cannot venture into maturity unless we realize the need and the purpose of who we are.

As mature Christians we will recognize our need for Christ. That He will bring us beyond our failures so we can grow increasingly effective for Him and grow in sanctification. We will be focused on the goal of holiness to be the person God created. He created us to be images of Himself, and as images we are to reflect His character, that goes beyond ourselves to the purpose He has. It is not about our needs but His needs, it is not our purpose but His purpose.

As we grow in Christ we will become aware of our futility and inadequacy as human beings, that we are products of our sin nature that only Christ can regain and redeem, and this frailty will become a strong building with the foundation of Christ and the power of the Holy Spirit who gives us extreme provision and realization to be our best for God's glory.

We become complete human beings who walk away from our fallen nature into a renewed nature in Christ. As we grow in the progress of our walk with Christ, we become more able to stay on the path of that He has for us. So that to open temptations and venture into new paths away from His presence will no longer consume our desires. Instead we are to become convicted to spiritual fulfillment that Christ has for us. Thus, when we walk on the path of God and we are confronted with the enormous assortment of doors all leading to temptations and desires, we will know what to do. All these distractions and sins leading away from His best for us will not be a temptation, but rather repulsive and ugly as they truly are.

With the power of the Holy Sprit and the conviction of faith in Christ, we are modeling His image with love. We are maturing. And the desires and aspirations that once hindered us will be of no bother, we will be able to walk away from them like a racehorse. A racehorse has its blinders on the side of its eyes, so it is always pointing straight ahead, so they are not distracted from leaving the course. We too must keep our eyes focused ahead so we are not distracted away from our Lord. For when we are overcome by our desires and distracted from our purpose, then the diseases will infect us like cancer and consume the body of Christ that ends up serving only our whims and the devils purpose. When we stop and open those doors of temptations, even the small doggie doors, we will be consumed and our growth in Christ will stop and the infection and diseases will replace their growth.

This temptation of distraction happens when we read the Word with the focus on ourselves. Thus with our devotions and prayer life being self-centered, we become distracted from the main purpose of our existence, that is to love and follow our Lord, and receive his redemption. When we become distorted from His plan by our willful disobedience, we leave His path for ours, and we get lost in our own desires and sins.

There are too many Christians who flat out and deliberately refuse to surrender themselves the Lordship of Christ. Christianity is merely fire insurance from Hell, or some means of social influence or personal desires that do not grow beyond the sinners prayer: Such as the parable of the sower.

Our Christian growth in maturity is not self-realization, but rather Christ realization. As we grow, we become totally aware of one great fact: there is one God and we are not it. That our confidence in who we are is because of the work Christ has done on our behalf. As we grow our utter dependence is upon our Lord and our confidence is in Him and not ourselves. Because people will always disappoint us, we will even disappoint ourselves, but Christ will not disappoint, but gives us the care, love, and His grace that we do not deserve. So we in turn model to others who we think do not deserve it or want it, because this is our mandate and call. {Excerpt from the book, "Pew Sitting" by Richard J. Krejcir}

Outline:

Remember to begin in prayer!

- Prayer   5 min
- Options and Story   5 min
- Read lesson and Bible passages   10-15min
- Discussion groups   15-30 min
- Going Deep   5-10 min
- Q & A, Application
- End in prayer.   5 min

Total lesson time 45 min—1 hr: {If you ad worship, which I strongly recommend, limit the discussion groups to the essential questions you feel they need. If your group is on the wild side, try some ideas from "Group Books," "Snoredom Busters," and "Boredom Busters." They take a couple of minutes and wake things up when youth or adults get bored!}

"Opening Story:" "The Graduation Present"

In a fairly wealthy family, the eldest son Niles was graduating from high school and was expecting a gift that he felt he deserved. All of his friends either already have brand new expensive cars or are about to get a brand new expensive car for graduation. He just spent the last three weeks looking at cars with his father, and picked out the one he wanted. Niles knew his father had to give him one, after all, all of his friends were getting one and he deserved it!

Niles had picked out the perfect car for college, it was a convertible and he knew he would be popular with it. So at the anticipated day, when the party was winding down, Niles opened his present from his father. Now the gift was eloquently wrapped in a box the size of a large book. Niles immanently thought it must be the keys and perhaps a book about his new car. So he carefully opened the present, as to preserve the nice paper and opened the box.

Suddenly Niles anticipation turned into rage, his longing and excitement became bitter and angry. It was a Bible! So he flipped through the pages and fanned it to see if any keys would fall out. Niles then tore through the wrapping, peered into the box, and nothing! Just a stupid worthless Bible with his name on it!

Niles could not believe it! He was so angry he threw the Bible at his father with a few colorful metaphors I cannot say. He stormed out of the house, as his father ran after him. His father never saw his son in person again!

Niles went to college and graduated, took whatever money he could get from his father, but flatly refused to talk to him or allow his father to explain what happened. Instead Niles chose to hold on to his bitterness like a warm coat on a cold night. Niles flatly refused to talk to his mother too, blaming her for allowing his father to embarrass him in front of his friends, and ruin his graduation.

Years latter Niles gets a call from his mother, his father was sick and wanted to talk to him, Niles refused, again choosing to hold on to his bitterness. A year later his mother called again, Niles quickly put her in her place, saying he did not want to talk to his father. His mother started to cry, and said it was too late, his father was no longer available to talk.

So Niles went home and, after the funeral was over, began to rummage through his father's things to see what he could get. After a couple of hours of rummaging, Niles found his high school graduation present. It was in the garage under an inch of dust. He could not believe it! He opened the driver's door and saw the bible on the front seat. He sat down and saw an envelope taped to the back cover he did not see years before. He opened it and it was a picture of his car with directions to the garage. And a note that said, "Son there is no gift greater that the story in this book, read it carefully and live a life worth living, a life centered on Christ."

God's desire is for us is to seek Him and not the stuff and things of the world. There is no gift greater than what Christ did, what is told to us in His Word?

"Seek ye first the kingdom of God, and His righteousness will come on to you." {Matt 6:33}

If we do not yield to it, if we do not open the gift given to us, we will live a life of bitterness and strife. A life that leads us to ruin, that no rich present could ever buy.

Optional opening, "Bible Quiz."

{You can copy this off to the students without the answers, have a student read them off, or play "Jeopardy" with them.}

Circle the quotes you think are false, be careful you may be surprised!

1. **The Bible is a story of our attempts to search for God.**
{False! It is a record of our fallen nature and God's choosing to redeem us.}

2. **The Bible proves the existence of God.**
{True, and proves our existence too!}

3. **All the books in the Bible are a response to God's love and care for His people.**
{True}

4. **The Bible is a scientific textbook describing the origin of the world.**
{True, it may not have all the details, but its accuracy is amazing, but also False because this is not the main theme of the bible just a facet.}

5. **The Bible is primarily a factual history of the Jewish people.**
{False, of all people}

6. **The Bible contains answers to all of humanity's problems and questions.**
{True; It may not tell us how to program the VCR, but all the essentials of our meaning and purpose and why we are here on the earth.}

7. **The Bible must be interpreted literally.**
{True and False; We need to interpret the Bible in its context, thus we do not need to literally gouge out our eye if we sin.}

8. **The main theme of the bible is the call to a moral and ethical life.**
{False; This would be the liberal interpretation, but the Bible is more than good living principles.}

9. **The Bible is a book of history without any application or lesson.**
{False, yes it is history but with insight meaning and lesson are for us today. If we do not learn from our past mistakes, we will learn nothing at all!}

10. **We must read the Bible like a spectator at a sports game and not as a participant.**
{False; It is our story, about our needs and nature and a God who loves and cares for His creation. Thus we need to read it as a participant, and definitely not as a spectator!}

11. **The Bible was written and produced all at once.**
{False; over 40 writers in a 1,500 year period of time!}

12. **Our job in studying the Bible is to learn to ask the right questions.**
{True and False; yes we need to ask the question, but also apply it!}

13. **There is no other important truth about God than what is disclosed in the Bible.**
{True; however Romans 1 tells us that God is revealed in His creation, which the Bible says, so the question is true!}

14. **The Old Testament has no meaning and truth for us today.**
{False; we cannot know the truth of the NT without understanding the OT.}

15. **The Bible is basically one story...that of God's redemption, that is His search for reconciliation with us, because of our fallen state.**

{True, This is the main theme, although there is a lot of other themes and truths too.}

16. Every book and chapter of the Bible has the same level of importance as every other book and chapter, [the Bible is a collection of
66 books].
{True; some parts may have more application and insight, but the
entire Bible is inspired and practical for us today.}

The Lesson: "The Importance of God's Word" {"Claims for the Bible"}

[Ideas on how to do this lesson so it does not come across boring:
Sometimes there is no better way to get facts out then just saying them.
So how can we do this without the sounds of snoring? First, believe with
passion what you are saying. Read through it thoroughly, and when you
are communicating to the younger crowed try to put things and ideas in
your own words. When you have a passion and like for the subject, that
excitement is contagious to those you are teaching.

What worked for me: Break down the parts and give a copy of the
lesson with the scriptures and "bullets" to the students to read.
Highlight each of their parts in advance. Read the primary outline
yourself, such as; "**Second: Christ's Claims For The Bible.**" While Jesus
Christ was on earth, He affirmed the Bible's claims for itself. In what He
said about it and in the way He used it, the Son of God showed the Bible
to be the Word of God. Consider the following:

Then have one student read: "Christ used the Bible and its stories as
fact, as history that applies to us today as it did then, that it has happened and will happen, thus Christ showed the Bible's authenticity and
accuracy."

Then another student read: "A. The commandment of God" (Mark
7:8).

This will keep it interesting and involve the students in the "Pedagogical" {lecturing} learning process, making it more "developmental"{getting the student involved in the learning process}. If you think of good questions yourself, go for it.

You can try this "mode" for most of the lessons.

"THREE REASONS TO TRUST THE BIBLE"

First: **The Bible's Claims For Itself.** The Bible claims, first of all, to be the Word of God to man:

"All Scripture is given by inspiration of God, and is profitable for doctrine, for reproof for correction, for instruction in righteousness." {I Timothy 3:16}

"Knowing this first, that no prophecy of Scripture is of any private interpretation [origin], for prophecy never came by the will of man, but holy men of God spoke as they were moved by the Holy Spirit." (II Peter 1:20-21)

These verses make a tremendous claim, they say that the Bible prophets did not just conjure up out of the air and originate what they wrote. Rather, they recorded what was given to them directly by God. They were moved (literally "borne along") by the Holy Spirit. Now that does not mean that their individual personality or style of writing was overpowered. It means that they were kept from having any error creep into what they wrote. And if it truly is what it claims to be—a God-inspired book then it is absolutely trustworthy.

Second: **Christ's Claims For The Bible.** While Jesus Christ was on earth, He affirmed the Bible's claims for itself. By what He said about it and in the way He used it, the Son of God showed the Bible to be the Word of God. Consider the following:

A. He used the Bible and its stories as fact, as history that applies to us and to those who went through, that it has happened and will happen, thus Christ showed its authenticity and accuracy:

"The commandment of God" (Mark 7:8)
"The Word of God" (Mark 7:13; John 10:35)
Jonah (Matthew 12:38-41)
Adam and Eve (Matthew 19:4-5)
Noah and the flood (Matthew 24:37-39)
"Scripture" (Luke 4:21; John 5:39, 10:35)
Lot, Lot's wife, and Sodom (Luke 17:28-32)

B. He saw His own words as Scripture to be believed and obeyed. (John 12:48-49)

C. He held people responsible for what was written in the Scriptures. (Matthew 12:3)

D. He used Scriptures as conclusive evidence in answering His critics:

Matthew 22:32 quoting Exodus 3:6, 15
Matthew 22:42-44 quoting Psalm 110:1

E. He used the authority of Scripture to refute the temptations of Satan in the wilderness. (Matthew 4:4-10)

Third: The Writers Claims For the Bible. The individual writers affirmed the Bible's claims for itself by accepting the other parts of the Bible as the Word of God. First let's look at how the Bible writers viewed the Scriptures:

- When Daniel read Jeremiah's prophecy that the Babylonian captivity would last 70 years, he accepted it as true and began to pray and plan accordingly. (Daniel 9:2)

- Peter accepted the supernatural origin of the writings in the Old Testament prophets and Paul's writings as scripture, even though he sometimes did not understand it.
  (II Peter 1:21) (II Peter 3:15-16)

- Secondly, the Biblical writers often saw themselves as communicating the Word of God. The prophet Isaiah began his book by proclaiming "For the Lord has spoken." (Isaiah1:2)

- The prophet Jeremiah opened his prophecy by saying, "Then the Word of the Lord came to me." (Jeremiah 1:4)

- God commissioned Ezekiel to go to His people and tell them "Thus says the Lord God." (Ezekiel 3:11)

- Paul claimed that the words he spoke were directly from God. (Galatians 1:11-12; 1 Thessalonians 2:13)

There are, of course, many more than "three reasons to trust the Bible." Among these are textual unity, textual preservation, historical accuracy, scientific accuracy, prophetic accuracy, and its social and personal impact. But even the above three reasons are enough to show that the claims the Liberals and cults make against the Bible are unfounded!

{This session was inspired in part from the book "Evidence that Demands a Verdict" by McDowell, and the booklet "Can I Really Trust the Bible?" published by Radio Bible Class Ministries.}

Discussion Questions for The Importance of Bible Study

Open Q: Have you ever taken a risk? If so what was it, and what happened?

1. Read Joshua 1:8; 24:14-15. Answer the following questions,

- What did these statements mean to Joshua?

- What risk could he have been taking?

- How can this statement, when applied to your life, make your life a difference?

- Why would studying God's Word be essential for our growth?

- What happens to Christians when they do not do as Joshua did?

2. Read Psalm 1, What are the benefits of studying God's Word?

{This does not mean problems will not come our way. But these verses do say that when we continue in His Word, we will be rich in fulfillment and meaning. Something that money, cars, popularity, cats, or anything can ever do! Just watch the VH-1 biographies of famous rock, TV and movie stars, and see how and what money fame and success did for them. 99% of the time they ended up dead from drugs, or totally frustrated and disillusioned with life. All that they had, which most of us can only dream about, could not bring them the deep fulfillment and happiness they desired!}

3. Are you like Niles in the story? Do you know anybody who is, without naming names? If so what do you think they will be like 10 years from now?

4. Was there anything new to you on the Bible Quiz?

Q: Was there anything that surprised you?

Q: What are your attitudes about the Bible in relation to this quiz, or in general?

5. Q: Are you confident that you know the Bible? Why or why not?

6. So if you had everything you ever wanted, what difference would that make? Would you end up like a Jim Morrison, Jimmy Hendriks, or Janis Joplin {Most popular rock stars of the 60's who all died by choking on their vomit, and died totally disillusioned and hopelessly unhappy.} or a Curt Corbain, who committed suicide at the height of his popularity a few years ago? How would their lives be different with God's Word?

7. Why did God give us the Bible?

8. So what will God's Word mean to you?

9. What will you do now that you know the importance of God's Word?

10. Do the three reasons make sense to you so that you can have more faith and trust in the Bible? If so, why is that important?

Application:

There are many ways in which we can trust in the Bible. So during the following week, look for and then write down things that are happening to you, such as problems, frustrations, decisions, and opportunities, and how the Bible could make the difference. Keep in mind, stress, anxiety, busyness, social impact and personal impact.

"GOING DEEP"

Have student's lay on the floor with the lights off and eyes closed. And ask them to see themselves as Joshua, and read the passages 1:8; 24:1-15. Then slowly in a contemporary paraphrase, such as the New Living Translation, or CEV, remain silent for 2 to 3 minutes and read vs. 16-18, and remind them that this is their story, you are there!

Ask; how did it feel to be Joshua? Could you actually see yourself there, why or why not? What did you see, what did you hear, what did you smell? Could you have been bold as Joshua and said and did as he did?

{You can cut down the discussion questions, and spend more time on this. Try it! You may think younger people such as high schoolers would not be interested. But my experience and the various other churches, which have tried this, have had excellent results, and it was received very well by the youth!}

Session II

Make "7-UP" Yours

Leaders Study:

The capable Bible student is rooted and grounded in the spiritual disciplines of the faith, whose drive is their passionate love relationship to the Lordship of Christ. And what flows out of it is the desire to love God's people, to herd them with love into the pastures of maturity. To lead where the leader has been before, and the people have not been. The mature Christian or leader must exhibit the maturity of the Christian life as the result of their growth and experience in the faith. An effective leader cannot be new to the faith. Even the Apostle Paul spent three years being discipled by Barnabas, and he received his call and was empowered directly from Christ Himself. I have seen too many immature Christians who lead by who they are in society, and not who they are in Christ.

A few years ago while on staff at a church, we received a family who came to faith at a crusade, and the father was the founder of a major fast food franchise. So in less than a year he was my boss, and the president and ruling Elder of the congregation. Now he was a great guy and very successful in business, but he did not know how to run a church. So he instinctually ran it like a business and his policies failed. He did not know how to lead in a church, which is different than in a corporation, even though a lot of the principles are transferable. After several years he did become a good leader as he matured in the faith. But the church suffered during his learning curve needlessly.

There is no substitute to time spent in the face of our Lord, with a surrendered heart and a learning will. We must be willing to be humble no matter who we are and our experience. I had to learn this lesson a few years back when I went from being on staff at a large and influential church to a small church in a small town. My first thought before accepting the call was that I was too good for it. But God wanted me there to teach me to walk closer to him, and not walk in the position that I held. So I did, and I experienced humbleness. Nobody knew me as the conference speaker or author or big position in a big church, but just a youth pastor in a small church. But this is where Christ wanted me, and I learned a lot. It prepared me for the road He had for me. And I'm glad I went there because I learned things in a broader context, that I could not have in a large "mega" church.

"Do your best to present yourself to God as one approved, a workman who does not need to be ashamed and who correctly handles the word of truth. Avoid godless chatter, because those who indulge in it will become more and more ungodly.

Flee the evil desires of youth, and pursue righteousness, faith, love and peace, along with those who call on the Lord out of a pure heart. Don't have anything to do with foolish and stupid arguments, because you know they produce quarrels. And the Lord's servant must not quarrel; instead, he must be kind to everyone, able to teach, not resentful." {II Timothy 2:15-16; 22-24}

This passage is a testimony to the importance of holiness, and to keep ourselves growing in our spiritual lives so that our emotional selves are impacted and grow too.

Spiritual maturity will lead into emotional maturity most of the time, unless there is some physiological or psychological problem, or deep stress that has never been resolved. It is imperative for the leader to be in control of their emotional health. If not, they need to step down and seek help both spiritually and psychologically. If the leader is given to fits of rage or is just overly emotional, they cannot set the example that Christ has. We are not to be Vulcan's exhibiting pure logic and no emotions, absolutely not. God created us as emotional beings, but as with anything we must have control of the excess and the potential for rampage.

Lesson Outline:

Remember to begin in prayer!

- Prayer   5 min
- Pick one of the options   5-10 min
- Read lesson and bible passages   10-15min
- Discussion groups   15-30 min
- Going deep   5-10 min
- Application   5 min
- End in prayer.

Total lesson time 45 min- 1 hr

Optional start up:

Play the song, "Aware of the Wonder" by Geoff Moore from the CD "Friend like You." After playing the song, read the words from the CD jacket.

- Ask what is the nature of God, and why does it lead us closer to Him?

Optional start up:

Read the poem from the beginning of the workbook. Read it slowly with their eyes closed. Ask them to visualize the words. After, explain some of the words if you have a younger audience:

"This book contains the mind of God, the state of man, the way of salvation, the doom of sinners, and the happiness of believers. Its doctrines are holy, its precepts are binding, its histories are true, and its decisions are immutable. Read it to be wise, believe in it to be safe, and practice it to be holy. It contains light to direct you, food to support you, and comfort to cheer you. It is the traveler's map, the pilgrim's staff, the pilot's compass, the soldier's sword, and the Christian's charter. Here paradise is restored, heaven opened, and the gates of hell disclosed. Christ is its grand object, our good its design, and the glory of God its end. It should fill the memory, rule the heart, and guide the feet. Read it slowly, frequently, and prayerfully. It is a mine of wealth, a paradise of glory, and a river of pleasure. It is given you in life, will be opened in the judgment, and be remembered forever. It involves the highest responsibility, will reward the greatest labor, and will condemn all who trifle with its sacred contents."

—-Author Unknown

{Try passing a photocopy with each clause highlighted, then have students take turns reading it as a story in the round}

The lesson: INTRODUCTION to the study of God's Word:
{Make "7-UP" Yours}

"Remember the Morning watch," it was the rallying cry on the Cambridge University campus in 1882. Several students' intent on growing deeper in their faith at a time when the popularity of Godly devotion was being replaced by scientific and liberal thinking. These students decided to take a stand in adversity and academic backlash. Their lives would echo as they do today on our public high school and college campuses. They found the harsh reality that Christianity was not an academic pursuit, instead filling their schedules with lectures, sporting events, studies, and student gatherings and so forth, just like we do today, but without TV!

The students found a fatal flaw in their busyness, even though they made a commitment to honor Christ: They had little time for the one they were honoring! As they described *"A crack in our spiritual armor, if not closed will bring us disaster!"*

So they sought an answer to their dilemma, a scheme to balance the hectic schedules and honor God. They came up with a plan called "The Morning Watch," that the first few minutes of the day will be dedicated to know the Lord.

One of the young men who was not fond of mornings devised a mechanical contraption with all kinds of levers and pulleys to persuade him out of bed! This idea spread like a wild fire and was used by God for a revival in England, which was depicted in the film "Chariots of Fire." The modern missionary movement was born as many Evangelical Ministries are still in existence today, such as YMCA and the Boy Scouts. Many famous pastors and missionaries who influenced many generations all stemming from giving God the first fruits of their day.

So will you meet this challenge?

The Challenge is simple, the idea is pure and practical and only requires your obedience and persistence! God desires our intimacy, our relationship, our communion with His holiness. Wow what an honor and opportunity to go before the holy Creator of the universe. Psalm 5:3; 57:7

So I challenge you to set aside time each day, the best time you have when you are the most alert and able to go before your creator and redeemer.

Start it off simple, say 7 minutes, and you can call it A7-UP!@ Seven minutes a day, seven days a week. Psalm 5:3

First pray for guidance, and prepare your heart and mind, take 2 minute.

Second read a passage from the "New Testament", and spend at least 4 minutes.

Third spend the rest of the 2 1/2 minutes in specific prayer. Such as your parents/family, school/work, people in your life, confession of your sins, and what you are thankful for. You may add the problems of our society, or spend it in silence and reverent mediation over the passage you just read, and that's it!

Then as you progress, you will have the desire to spend even more time. Most committed Christians will spend more then an hour in prayer each day plus time in scripture. You say you do not have the time? Well many Christian leaders do it and they have schedules that would blow yours away! There is always time, the question is will you make it?

So when the morning watch comes...

Discussion Questions "INTO THY WORD"

Open Q: When you are at a bookstore and see a lot of books that say "The Complete Bible of Computer Knowledge" or "The Bible of Facts" etc. How does this make you feel; does it cheapen the real Word of God?

1. Will you be willing to make a commitment to the "Morning Watch?"

2. What is it like to share your faith at your campus or work?

3. Does popularity and fear to offend have a bearing on how you model the character of Christ, or be His witness?

4. What were the young men faced with on the Cambridge campus?

5. Have you ever faced a similar dilemma?

6. Could you see yourself facing it in the future, why or why not?

7. What flaws are in your life? And what can you do about them?

8. Have you ever been apart of something that just took off, a fad or following a commitment?

9. What specific things do you have to do in your life to make "7-UP" work? "Make 7-up yours?"

10. So what are you going to do when the alarm clock sounds?

Application:

Make a commitment if you are willing to stay with it on the "Morning Watch."

Now if you are not a morning person, pick another time and stick with it. Use the "90 Day Experience" By Jim Burnes, or a "One year Bible" as your scripture guide. This may make the 7 minutes more like 15, if this is too long to start off with, cut in half.

Going Deep:

Spend 7 minutes practicing the morning watch. Assign the passage Philippians 3. Turn off the lights for 3 minutes of dead silence and ask students to ponder their passage. Then close in prayer.

SESSION III

"Getting away from Distractions!"

Leaders Study: "ATTITUDE"

Do you call yourself an expert on receivership? You probably say What? Or no way! But do you live your life this way, having a "me first" identity, always placing the emphases on the "I" and "Me." If only I... If it could go this way for me...Then I could....

"I have been crucified with Christ and I no longer live, but Christ lives in me. The life I live in the body, I live by faith in the Son of God, who loved me and gave himself for me." {Gal 2:20}

This means that the ownership of your life is completely self focused and centered. The ownership of your life is yours and yours alone! But Christ calls us to Him, and out of ourselves. Our ownership has been transferred, our pink slip has been signed over from ourselves to Christ, IF you postulate Christ as your Lord. What effect are you having to those around you? When we relinquish ourselves to Christ, then the proper attitude of life will take over. The vision of our life and the result of what we have will be based on a positive outlook. A positive attitude that is based solely on what Christ has done for us. So regardless of our external circumstances, we are to be totally focused on our Lord. We then are to allow our attitudes to be Christ centered. We could allow our circumstances to take the lead or Christ to take the lead, the choice is given to us.

If we are receivership oriented and not Christ centered, then all of those circumstances will be squeezed, and bitterness and resentment will flow out of them. Or we can be Christ centered and oils of sweetness will pour out. What pours out from you? Is it the love and care that is modeled to those around us or bitterness and hostility. Bitterness will not be squeezed from our circumstances, but from our attitude, which results from those circumstances. The way Christ is exhibited in you will be from your focus and attitude and not your circumstances. Your direction in life, your joy and happiness, your cares and concerns, your willingness to reach beyond yourself will grow from your attitude and maturity, all stemming from who you are in Christ!

The circumstance will change once we realize our wrong thinking and error. The receivership mentality dies within us and the Christ centered life is birthed. This is the way we are made, the reason we endure suffering, the way a fallen, sinful, and unjust world is turned from the glory of Satan into the glory of our Lord. We do this by allowing Christ to reach in us and conform us to His image and character, regardless of what we are going through, regardless of our circumstances. As we raise Christ up in our thinking and in our attitude, it changes who we are and what we do. So that we are people of distinction by our perceived behavior by others from a changed core of who we are by what Christ has done!

The attitude will be the impact that strikes at the issues of life, breaking them away from our hurt and pain to the absorption of grace and the acceptance of Christ. We can not trust in our education, wealth, success, failures, people, appearances, skill, gifts, or circumstances. The attitude of trusting in things and circumstances must be laid on the floor of the cross and no where else. So the attitude of trust in Christ takes over who we are. Our attitude must be Christ driven and not appearances driven. We must embrace the day with joy, knowing Christ is at work in us, in those around us.

Life is 10% what happens to us and 90% how we react to it. As the elect, saved by grace, it is still up to us what we make out of what Christ gives us. Maturity will make the difference of a life of distinction and purpose, or a life governed by strife and chaos. So what is your response? What is your attitude? Where does your maturity lay?

Lesson Outline:

Remember to begin in prayer!

- Prayer   5 min
- Pick one of the options   5-10 min
- Read lesson and bible passages   10-15min
- Discussion groups   15-30 min
- Going deep   5-10 min
- End in prayer and repeat application.   5 min

Total lesson time 45 min—1 hr

Open Activity:

Have your group sit in a circle and say, "Once upon a time," then have each person take turns clock wise to finish the story. Each person just puts in a sentence or two, and the next person takes it and so forth. Have your students use their imaginations, it may be funny or serious, let the story continue for 5 or so minutes.

Explain that even Shakespeare, the most eloquent writer in the history of the English language, was not able to create a unifying theme throughout his works. Nor was he able to give them application and meaning for life. Although it is a wonderful look into the human condition, in the end they are just great plays and sonnets {love poems} that cannot save us.

The Bible took over 1500 years and over 40 known authors to complete God's masterful work. From Genesis through Revelation we have a universal theme of the fall of man, God's love for us and His pursuit for our regeneration {He saved us from our sinful nature and guilt by His shed blood of grace}. The Bible is a complete testimony of the human condition, the story and meaning for our existence, and the meaning of life.

Optional Story: "Grandpa's Attitude"

{This is a great illustration that I personally have seen in various forms over the years. This is a copulation of several stories of people beating the odds.}

Matt was a slow, awkward, and clumsy kid. He was shorter than the rest of the kids, had a speech impediment, and could not walk a straight line growing up. His grandfather was an Olympic athlete years ago and Matt wanted to be just like him, but was told by his parents and teachers it could never happen.

So Matt tried and tried to play sports, to run, to hit the ball or receive a pass. All Matt could do was look ridiculous and make the other kids tease and chase him. But Matt was determined to find a sport he was good at. His grandfather was a big source of encouragement and told Matt to never let people tell you that you cannot do something. It is your attitude that will determine your outcome over any ability you may or may not have.

So with his grandfather's support, he decided to keep plugging away through the teasing, failures, and setbacks he experienced. Soon he got the attention of his high school track coach who noticed that he could run. Matt never considered track; he wanted to play baseball or football. You see, Matt was like a "Forrest Gump," always teased and chased after. So out of sheer need, he developed great running skills.

Matt's grandfather bought him a letterman's jacket and said it was his as soon as you make the track team, even though his mother was outraged that her father was setting Matt up to fail. Matt knew he could do it. So he practiced every day, but when he tried out, he did not make the freshman cut. So Matt kept on practicing, and his grandfather kept on encouraging and his mother and classmates kept on teasing and harassing him. Matt persevered.

Two weeks before the junior varsity tryouts, Matt's grandfather died. Matt's mother knew this would be the end of her son's pipe dream and feared he would be devastated. Yes Matt was, and feared all of his work would be for nothing, because his grandfather would not be there. But he remembered his grandfather telling him he is to do it for himself and no one else.

Matt's Mom comforted him and said to him that he should give up. She loved him and just did not want her son to experience any more humiliation. But Matt pressed on and entered the meets for the tryouts. Matt made the cut! And he was not even at the bottom, but right in the middle of the group and would be a starter on the sprints!

His coach called Matt over and gave him a large envelope. Matt opened it and saw the school letter for his jacket along with a note from his grandfather that read, "Matt I knew you could do it."

Matt had someone to encourage and believe in him. We have a God who made us, gifted us, and loves us. He gives us the ability and strength to press on to the goal that we are called to do. The ability may not be ours but the choice to pursue it and the attitude that goes with it is our choice to make.

God has an envelope for us too, will we reach for it with a winner attitude or become bitter and withdrawn as Matt could easily have done? The choice is ours. But beware, a life with a bad attitude will be a life filled with strife, conflict, sleeplessness, and unhappiness. We are to pursue a "Rad Dude Attitude" no matter what we are going through, God will bless and keep us, and we will be that Rad Dude or Dudess!

Lesson: "Getting away from Distractions!" {"Having a Rad Dude attitude"}

This series is meant to be a simple guide to help you dig into God's Word. It will provide you with the "map" of questions, tools, and a chart; but you must provide the will. To surrender our will to God's will is the essential element of being a growing Christian. God's Word provides the way; you simply provide the means.

There are many ways we can study the bible effectively. There is no "best" way, only that we do it! Many Christians feel all they have to do for Bible lessons is sit in a pew, turn on the television or radio, or naturally receive their knowledge for being a Christian; but this is not how to transform our lives. We must read and get into the Word of God ourselves: Through prayer, hard work, discipline, concentration, application, and even more **prayer!**

So set aside time each day free from distractions and go for it with passion and vigor. Let Christ transform you through His Word.

"For the Word of God is quick and powerful, and sharper than any two edged sword, piercing even to the dividing asunder of soul and spirit, and the joints and marrow, and is discerner of the thoughts and intents of the heart." {Hebrews 4:12 KJV}

PRELUDE INTO GOD'S TREASURE CHEST:

ATTITUDE: Start with the proper attitude! You are going before a Holy God, so adjust yourself with these attitudes:

REVERENCE: {Hab. 2:20, Psalm 89:7} Prepare your heart and mind, you are not going to a football game! Be quiet; clear your distracting thoughts and desires away!

YOUR WILL: {John 7:17f} We must be willing to not only read but to obey God's decrees! It is not about you, it is about God! Make it your choice!

ANTICIPATION: {Psalm 63:1} We must come before God with eagerness and expectancy. This is not a chore; it is fellowship with the creator of the universe, what better time could there be!

BE ALERT: {Prov. 1:7; 3:5-6} Find a time where you are most alert and awake!

BE IN LOVE: {Job 23:12; Jeremiah. 15:16} Fall in love with His Word! Have the appetite, as it was better than your favorite meal! Do not let it be just a duty! The love will increase as we increase in our effort and study!

"Open my eyes that I may see wonderful things in your law." {Psalm 119:18}

A very important point: For this to work, you must have a relationship with Christ, with your trust in His grace. Without it you are programming a computer without any knowledge of its language or design. You may attempt it, but all you will get is *"foolishness;"* as Scripture tells us, the knowledge will be hidden from you.

"The man without the Spirit does not accept the things that come from the Spirit of God, for they are foolishness to him, and he cannot understand them, because they are spiritually discerned. The spiritual man

makes judgments about all things, but he himself is not subject to any man's judgment." {I Cor. 14-15}

In God's eyes it is far more important **why** we do something than that we do something, even good. {I Sam 16:7, II Chron. 25:2} Thus we do not want to do the right thing with the wrong attitude and motives.

Discussion on "INTO THY WORD"

Open: Have all the students tie each other's wrists behind them with masking tape, so they cannot move their hands. The teacher will have to read the Bible passages. They cannot try to break free and must remain sitting down! Do not tell them why they are being tied!

1. What is it like not to be able to move your hands?

2. Read Hebrews 4:12 in several versions if available. Explain that this imagery is like an animal being cut opened and the guts coming out! {Girls should like this one}
   Q. Why does the Bible use this imagery to describe itself?

3. How can the Word of God get into you so you become divided and everything is exposed in you? {Explain the importance of surrendering our will, so God can use us. He usually does not when we get in the way.}

4. How can you develop a good attitude, and why would that be important in life as well as bible study?

5. Why is reverence so important, what does it mean to you?

6. Why should we be alert?

7. What happens when we do something such as operate heavy machinery or drive a car when we are not alert?

8. Have you ever set aside time to do devotions and read the Bible by yourself on your own accord?

9. If so, how did it go? How long did you last?

10. If you stopped, why and what would be the essential ingredient [s] to keep plugging away at it?

11. How powerful is God's Word in your life?

12. Have you ever anticipated something real bad? What was it like to anticipate? How did you feel when you received the anticipated answer?

13. See scriptures I Sam 16:7 & II Chron. 25:2: Why is it more important to have a **why** to do good stuff instead of "just do it?"

Application:

Place a $5 bill on the table in front of the students {do not expect it back} and ask them to try to get it without breaking their masking tape cuffs. Explain having a negative attitude is cutting them off from the blessings and wonder that God has in store for them. You may not be rich or famous, but that is not important, it is the positive attitude of life and receiving His redemption and blessing that will give you meaning and true happiness that no car, job, house, spouse or anything that could ever bring you!

Negative attitudes will tie us up from experiencing life, joy, fulfill-ment, peace, love and happiness! Negative attitudes will also get in the way of refusing to give our will up for our Lord and savior. Go through the next week being fully aware of your attitudes, keep a journal of them, that is keep track of your negative attitudes and positive attitudes. Then notice your feelings and responses in those situations.

Going Deep:

"Prayer Walk." Spend as much time as you can, or schedule this at a different time, maybe after church, or before church next week, instead of games for youth group, etc.

Go to a public place such as a shopping mall and greet people at ran-dom and say something nice and uplifting.

{Do not witness your faith for this exercise. You can and should at a different time, because it will give you much different results. Maybe have 2 of your group witness, and the other 2 just greet. Try it!} At the same time be praying silently for the people you are talking too. Notice the attitudes of the people you are encouraging, and notice your atti-tude as people return kindness or bitterness. Keep in mind how you can be a bitter free person who is an encourager to others.

SESSION IV

"God's Love Letter"

Leaders Study: "What Love is" {I Corinthians 13:1-8}

This passage is our template on how we must behave towards one another and towards those around us. We can do our best in preaching the gospel with power and conviction, and have a church filled with wonderful programs and staffed with gifted people. We can be in a magnificent cathedral reaching upwards and manifesting and pointing to the glory of God; but, if we're doing it to ourselves and not out of love, we accomplished nothing. We become just an annoying noise to our neighbors who we are called to reach. The proper use of our abilities and gifts as a Christian is always within the parameters of love. When a computer is programmed, the program runs because the language has instructed what the program is to do. Within this language of computers there are things called parameters which tell the program what it can and cannot do, thus the program can only operate within its own guidelines called parameters. We must look at this passage as our parameter, as our guideline and how we must execute the gifts, exercise the passion, and proclaim the truth.

What Love Means

This passage tells us the way of our Christian life and walk. As Christians, we imitate Christ, and work within His parameters which is love. This passage is a character description of who Christ is, and this passage must also be our character description of how we act and behave responsibly.

When God tells us that love is patient, He means we are to give others room to grow, and time to accomplish the work that God is doing in them. When someone is abrupt with us, or someone treats us wrongly we are called to be patient because we cannot have everything our way all the time. We cannot allow ourselves to become angry when others fail to our expectations that we set for them. Because God is patient with us and God loves us, we are to show patience with others. We need to be content and not become angry, for this is love: love never gives up.

When God tells us that love is kind, He means we are to look for the best in other people. We spend our energies and time encouraging and building up each other, and not tearing them down. You see God takes our circumstances of life and builds them in a constructive way for personal growth and are for better use toward each other. God does not treat us as an object to be manipulated and controlled because He has given us free will. So we should do the same with each other. Therefore, we always need to be seeking the healing of relationships, and be cautious in our judgments toward others. Love cares more about others than it does for ourselves.

When God tells us that love does not envy, He means we need to be happy for who we are. So when we hear that a friend receives a promotion before we do, we are to be happy for them. If we have a sibling who excels better than we are, we should be happy with them. If our neighbor has a brand new car, we should be happy for them, and be thankful for the old wreck that we may drive. That is we are to be happy for someone else who has something we don't have even if we don't like it.

So we do not become possessive and control freaks, especially in our relationships. Being possessive and controlling others will destroy a church very quickly, or the very least neuter its effectiveness. Love does not desire which it does not have.

When God tells us that love does not boast, He means we are not to go around bragging about our accomplishments and abilities. We are not to go around showing off our possessions. In doing so, we are condescending to those who do not have such things. We are not to be so full of our own accomplishments, we fail to see what others have accomplished too. Because God loves us so much we should have no need to impress each other, but allow God to impress us with his greatness because He is God and we are not. We can relax and enjoy who we are in Christ, since we do not have to be in control or be the life of the party to feel secure. Love does not strut around.

When God tells us that love is not proud, He means we must be willing to be in relationships with all kinds of people especially those outside our perceived race. We do not let our fears hold us back from one of life's most precious gifts: friendship. Not being proud means that when we make a mistake, we own up to it and admit that we are wrong even when we feel we aren't. Because God loves us, He is on our side and wants us to grow and mature in His love. We do not have to have an inflated ego about the perceived importance of ourselves. We need to seek others first and their well being, and not our arrogance and egocentric mentality. Love does not parade itself.

When God tells us that love is not rude, He means that we treat others with the respect and dignity that we would like in return. Because God loves us, He sent his Son to cover us and protect as from His wrath, thus when we make the mistakes that we do, even the big mistakes, we are not zapped by lightning bolts. So in return, we should not go around zapping others with evil looks and condescending comments, thinking that we are high and mighty and better than everyone else. Never think of yourself as the Capstone and the most important piece of the puzzle, because you're not. We should be grateful that God uses us, and our goal is to work together; and not be little dictators. Love does not force itself.

When God tells us that love is not self-seeking, He means that we place others first and not ourselves. That we are to be considerate, appreciative, not critical, and dignified as good manners would dictate to one another. Because God loves us so much, He did not have a self-seeking attitude, for if He did He would never have sent His Son on our behalf. Every Christian must respect the rights and dignity of other people and never force our will and thoughtless behaviors on others. We need to be happy when others around us experience success and growth, and never be jealous. Love does not have a "me first" attitude.

When God tells us that love is not easily angered, He means just that. We are to become very slow to get angry, and we do not let little things cause us to fly off the handle. Because God loves us so much, He did not allow His anger to wipe us out of existence when we so much deserved it. Instead He allowed His drama of redemption to unfold throughout history climaxing with Christ. We need to try to understand other people, and place ourselves in each other's shoes respectfully. We need to listen and not allow our hostile feelings to get the best of us. Since God is patiently working in us, we should reciprocate with the understanding of the debt we have to God and the unfathomable love and concern He has for us. Love is not touchy, resentful, and does not fly off a handle.

When God tells us that love keeps no record of wrongs, He means we don't go around with a list writing down the faults of each other. Rather we are to look for the positive things that happen in our relationships and affirm people. We do not go around with a negative attitude; but, one that is positive and equipping to God's people. Because God loves us so much, He does not keep a scorecard of our sins as long as we honestly repent from them. We do not need to reflect and gossip about the flaws of other people so to elevate ourselves, when God refuses to do it to us. Love does not keep a scorecard.

When God tells us that love does not delight in evil, He means we don't enjoy when bad things happen to others. We not only need to enjoy doing bad things to each other, but we refuse to allow evil to happen. We should feel bad when we see others being hurt. Compassion is one of God's great characteristics, and we should strive our fullest to model it to each other. Because God loves us so much, He is deeply grieved when we do not follow His example and His will. We are not to put others down, so to make ourselves feel good about ourselves. Love does not delight in evil.

When God tells us that love rejoices in truth, He means when we see injustice corrected, and people treating others with respect, kindness, and honestly, we should feel wonderful. Because God loves us so much, we should live our lives so that it reflects a God of truth and justice. Thus, we should find delight when we see justice being played out in others. As Christians, we should get excited when justice prevails, and we should be mad when injustice occurs and people's rights are violated. We should realize how much God rejoices when we personally stand up to the pressures of life and prevail with integrity and truth. Love takes pleasure in truth.

When God tells us that love always protects, He means we should feel protected and in return protect those around us. This does not mean we become security guards, it means our actions and attitudes are such that they project protection, and not destruction. Because God loves us so much, He does not forsake us, even though others may. People will always disappoint us, and we will always disappoint those around us; but God will never disappoint us. Love perseveres, and is the easier route than running off and abandoning our relationships, which we have committed to. We should realize how much God grieves when we fail to walk the life of His path and when we do not trust His protection. Love is always on the lookout and has staying power.

When God tells us that love always hopes, then we should be assured He will give us a future. We should be assured that when things are going bad, they will always get better. There is hope because our circumstances will always change. We should never lose hope. Because God loves us so much, He always has hope for us. God is patiently working in us, and when we understand what God has truly done for us, then we should have as much hope as we could ever need. We should see the potential in other people, what they can accomplish and become, and not hold them back out of our jealously. Love always is enduring and points to the future.

When God tells us that love always perseveres, He means for us to hang in there and keep going strong. Because God loves us so much, He will stand with us, and even carry us through our difficulties and strife. Even when we feel we have reached rock bottom, have no hope, and filled with despair, God is carrying us because He loves us. This is the love that will destroy rumors and gossip and cause us to believe the best about each other until proven otherwise by facts. Love refuses to quit. {Excerpt from the book, "Pew Sitting" by Richard J. Krejcir}

Lesson Outline:

Remember to begin in prayer!

- Prayer   5 min
- Pick one of the options   5-10 min
- Read lesson and bible passages   10-15min
- Discussion groups   15-30 min
- Going deep   5-10 min
- End in prayer and repeat application.   5 min

Total lesson time 45 min- 1 hr

Optional start up:

Get several books on various subjects and age levels from your church library or home. Start off with the simplest book and ask how hard will it be to master the knowledge in this book? And keep doing this to each book, from children's, juvenile, textbook, technical computer manual, etc. You can have the youth rate them on a scale of 1 to 10. Then the last book, hold up the Bible, and get the biggest King James you can find. It may get the 10 as the hardest. Explain to the students that God's Word is fully knowable and usable at all age levels. The more you study the Bible, the more you will know. It is practical and knowable, even more so than the simplest children's book because those books will not renew and save you. A health book may change your life, but God's Word will change you for eternity!

Optional start up:

Have students creatively act out as a skit or melodrama each of the attitudes listed: 1. "me first" identity, 2. always placing the emphasis on the "I" and "Me." 3. If only I... If it could go this way for me...Then I could. 4. Being conceited and condescending to others. Or create your own melodrama.

Lesson: "God's Love Letter"

When we try to live the Christian life alone without the guidance and support from the Word, we are like a pilot of an airplane flying through thick clouds who then refuses to admit that they have vertigo and continues to fly upside down!

As a Christian, we need to live a life of distinction, and the only way to receive the knowledge of that distinction is to get into the Word! We do not want to be "bar-code" Christians who, do not care what's in the box only the label that

matters, or that Christianity is just "fire insurance" from hell!

We must seek out the truth and answers that we need, from the final authority, and not the ways of the world! **If not then we set up ourselves as the final judge and authority and not God,** thus we will lead ourselves to hell from false truths and distractions.

The Response of grace and the point of Christianity is to be a transformed person, through self-surrender to our Lord's holiness through His Word and prayer!

REMEMBER: *THE BIBLE IS GOD'S LOVE LETTER TO YOU!!!*

- We need to get into the Bible ourselves. One of the problems of Christianity today is that we are conditioned to be taught from the scriptures but not to do it for ourselves.

- The cults place their authority elsewhere, and not in the Word!

The study of the Bible matters!

Because it brings us inline to His Holiness, and with reality! Science may have explanations, but they change completely every few years, however the Word of God never changes, what a great comfort!

Science can never explain love, justice, peace, goodness, purity, sin…because you cannot quantify it in a microscope or scientific instrument! *"Why we do what we do,"* cannot be scientifically measured and hypothesized, that is why there are so many theories in science and psychology and they are always changing!

- The Bible is read much, but studied little!

- The truths of Scripture will transcend any other subject, discipline or passion!

The Bible gives us a greater reality that can not be seen but is clearly felt, and to deny it is like living in Huntington Beach in southern California and never seeing the ocean!

- **The point of Christianity** is to be a transformed person, through self-surrender to our Lords holiness through His Word and prayer!

- **The Response of grace** is to be a transformed person, through self-surrender to our Lord's holiness through His Word and prayer!

Discussion Questions:

Q: When you hear the word "BIBLE" what comes to your mind first? Did love letter come to anyone?

1. Have you ever received a love letter? How did you feel? Have you ever written one?

2. What do you think is the best way to go about the study of scripture?

3. Have you ever been through a difficult or confusing situation where you did not know which end is up?

4. How did you respond?

5. Was God the focus, and was the Word consulted?

6. If not what difference would it make?

7. What specific things can you do to make your devotions a joy instead of a chore?

8. What does it mean to live a life of distinction? What happens when you do not?

9. What do you think about the statement; "If God's Word is not your final authority, then you set yourself up as the final authority and judge of life. This will lead your straight to Hell! False truth and distractions of life will lead you away from God's love and care to a life of unfulfillment and strife!"

10. How does this sit with you?

11. What will you do about it?

12. Read the following scriptures and compare it to these following statements:

HEB 4:12   EPH 6:17   ISA 55:11   MAK 4:1-9
JAM 1:21-25   MAT 7:24   JOHN 4:9-14

• Because the Bible is a "SWORD." Heb 4:12. Living and powerful. Thus Jesus is living, Jesus is sharp and will cut and penetrate our hearts. It will open us up from the inside out to reveal our nakedness and impurity!

• Since the Bible is a sword, it is a weapon that can and will defeat the dark forces against us, so we must know it to be able to use it! Eph 6:17

- Because the Bible is a "TACTICAL WEAPON." Isaiah 55:11 You can aim it for specific purposes.

- Because the Bible is a "SEED." Mark 4:1-9 A small but powerful word can make a big miracle in the heart and actions of the Bible student. And will only grow under the right soil conditions of our will!

- Because the Bible is a "MIRROR." James 1:21-25 It will reflect what is in our hearts and minds! It will show you the truth. Will you accept it?

- Because the Bible is a "ROCK." Matt 7:24-29 The foundation for our life and work. It is essential for us to build anything relevant and purposeful. Without it, we are building on sand that will wash us away! Without it, we will be unable to withstand the pressures of life and the call Christ gives us!

- Because the Bible is "LIVING WATER." John 4:9-14 It is the fountain we are to drink from!

- Because the Bible is our "BREAD." I Pet 2:1-3 It is our spiritual food, and we are what we eat!

- Because the Bible is the record of God speaking!

Application:

- Never tease a weasel or put ferrets in your pants {just good stuff to know}!

- Know the importance and relevance of Scripture {the real point}!

Going Deep:

"Practicing Silence." Have students spread out and remain totally quite with no thoughts for 5 minutes. Then bring them back and close by reading Psalm 1 in a paraphrase.

This lesson will help to learn solitude and not to be so cluttered with our own thoughts that we have no room for God.

SESSION V

"The Bible is a greater Reality"

Leaders Study: *"holiness"*

If someone said the word *"holiness"* to you, what would come to your mind first? You'd probably associate holiness with God. But did you ever stop to think about what God's holiness is all about?

What does the Bible mean when it says, *"Holy, holy, holy is the LORD Almighty"* (Isaiah 6:3)?

The word "holy" is translated in from the Old Testament and it means, "separated" or "cut apart." God is holy because He is totally, completely, and absolutely separate from everything He has ever created because He cannot be infected by sin! He is a cut above everything in the universe.

He is perfect, pure, and separate from the slightest hint of sin, error or evil. Can you visualize perfection in your life, that is living out a totally perfect sinless existence? It is not easy, is it? What about purity? That's just as difficult. Have you ever wondered how we are to understand God's holiness if we can't picture what it means?

Well God provided a Way for us to understand Him, a model for us to follow. Jesus said, *"Anyone who has seen me has seen the Father."* (John 14:9) If we want to "see" the holiness of God more clearly, we need to look at the life of Jesus Christ. Jesus was holy in that He was perfect. He never made a mistake. He never miscalculated or judged incorrectly. He always did the right thing at the right time in the right way

Jesus was holy in that He was and is pure. He never sinned (can you imagine that?). Yes, He walked among sinners. He mingled with them, ate with them, laughed with them, cried with them, healed them, and loved them. But He never became attached to their sinful attitudes or actions. And, with love and care, He called them to leave their lives of sin (John 8:11). God is like that.

But that's not all. Our holy God Expects us to be holy too: *"But just as he who called you is holy, so be holy in all you do; for it is written: 'Be holy, because I am holy."* (1 Peter 1:15-16)

Now we can say this is a tough standard, but does this mean we do not try because it is so tough? Thus if we never reach it, why bother with it? A lot of Christians live their lives this way. So they never try, but we must try anyway. We can get closer to God's standard of holiness every day by relinquishing ourselves to Christ in our prayers, devotions, and relationships. And we can rejoice in the fact that a day is coming when we will stand in God's presence as holy people singing *"Holy, holy, holy is the LORD Almighty"!!!!*

So let us go out and live as our life belongs to our Lord, as it does, and be holy!

Lesson Outline:

Remember to begin in prayer!

- Prayer   5 min
- Pick one of the options   5-10 min
- Read lesson and bible passages   10-15min
- Discussion groups   15-30 min

- Going deep 5-10 min
- End in prayer and repeat application.   5 min

Total lesson time 45 min- 1 hr

Optional Start up:

- If you did not use the bible Quiz in Session 1, then do it. Do not spend too much time on it:

Ask:

Q: Was there anything new to you on the Bible Quiz?

Q: Was there anything that surprised you?

Q: What are your attitudes about the Bible in relation to this quiz, or in general?

Q: Are you confident that you know the Bible? Why or why not?

Optional Start up:

Be very discerning and ask the pastor and or elders before you do this one! Bring in a weapon, which is completely unloaded and non-functional, preferably an antique. You can make a "papier-mâché," mace, or? Or have a police officer come in to your class.

Ask the students what is this device used for?

Let them touch it and hold it, {if expectable}

Ask how is the Bible like a weapon?

The lesson: "The Bible is a greater Reality"

{Have students take turns reading each stanza, and another read the Bible verse.} Read Psalm 19 in a good translation such as the NIV.

- We cannot believe and trust in Christ without the knowledge from the Bible, because it is our primary source material.

- If the Bible is in doubt, then all of our faith rests in mud and has no foundation to stand on, that is why a high view of scripture is essential to the growing believer!!

- As you can see, the Word of God is essential to our function as a Christian. It is essential to our understanding of not only God, but ourselves as well.

- Without God's word, we will be purposeless and disrupted from our call and the purpose for our salvation.

- When we base our lives on the Word of God, then Christ can create His work in us by the power of the Spirit!

- VALUE IS A MATTER OF WORTH, SO WHAT IS IT WORTH TO YOU?

- The Bible brings us into the reality of life!

- The world is a material temporary entity, we are being formed for eternity!

- The Bible is a greater reality than what is seen!

Discussion Questions

Sit back and close your eyes, {No we will not do anything mean to you!} and visualize your spiritual pilgrimage, that is growth from the earliest time you can remember up to now.

- What is your first memory of God?
- What was the highest time in your relationship with God?
- What was the lowest time?

Now on a piece of paper draw a graph by years since you where born until today, and mark the ups and downs. Do another graph using the same years and chart how you treated people, your family, your friends, people at church, and strangers?

- What do you see? {Usually there is a direct correlation between how we treat people with love, care, dignity and respect and how good our relationship with Christ is. When we treat Christ well, we then in turn treat others well too.}

Why would this be important in the study of God's Word?

1. When did you first read the Bible for yourself, on your own accord?

2. Why would prayer be so important and essential to the mystery chest of scripture?

3. What happens when we read the Bible and set up a barrier between us and the Word of God, that is getting our will in the way of God's?

4. A complaint by Biblical scholars is that today's youth see faith, the Word, and their spiritual life as a buffet. Where you can pick and choose your beliefs and ideas by the outward appearance of its package, unconcerned what is actually in the box, unconcerned what is truth and validity. So, how do you feel about this statement, is it true for you or your friends, or people you know?

5. Have you experienced the Bible as a sword or a mirror, where it pointed out a sin or convicted you?

6. Have you ever experienced anything supernatural, or heard of someone who has? Would you be scared? Why or why not?

7. How would the Bible give you comfort?

8. Have you ever used the Bible for a specific purpose, such as look up something you did not know? Was your question/quest answered?

9. Has your faith grown in the last year, and if so what part did the Bible play?

10. When you read the Bible do the characters jump out to you so that you see yourself in them or others that you know?

11. Why is the Bible a rock or a foundation for our living? What happens when we neglect it?

Now you may be thinking I know all of this stuff, why are we doing this! Well do you get it? Have you set times to read the Bible on a daily basis? Do you look to it when you are struggling with an issue or a problem, or a decision to make? You may intellectually get it but the getting has not reached your will and the rest of your body! It is not a matter of just knowing something, it has to reach the core of your being of who you are, the existential core of "you" before you will see any changes or passion or differences in your life and others!

12. So do you get the fact that the Bible is essential to all of life's understanding and happenings?

13. What would your life be like without it?

Application:

Think through how the Bible can be your reality. How you can be formed in it's image, that of the character of Christ. That you stand out from the crowd, at a time of your life when it is considered "uncool." Even your Christian friends may think you are weird by having regular devotions and living a life of distinction. Distinction does not happen when you are with your families on Sunday only!

• So what can you do NOW, TODAY, and NEXT WEEK to implement the reality of the bible in your life?!?!?

Remember you are a person who is deeply loved and fully accepted by our LORD!!!

"Going Deep"

Read Psalm 19 in the "Message" or other paraphrase. Read it slow in the dark by candlelight. Then remain silent for three minutes.

LESSON VI

"FIND OUT FOR YOURSELVES!!!"

Teachers Study: "desires"

Our desires must be focused on Him: Christ our Lord. We must feel the anticipation and the excitement to be with and in Him, so that we not only hear His Word; but we do His Word, the Word of God. So if we become stuck in our anxious thoughts, confusion, or the stressed out urgency of life, we stop and get our focus right! Pray that the Holy Sprit intercedes in you and removes the disruptions. Allow yourself to receive His comfort and grace. Remember it is not anything we do or effort on our part, we are only to receive what Christ our Lord gives us. And to receive, we need to make sure stuff that gets in the way, are out of the way.

Augustine, a "Catholic Saint," was one of the foremost philosophers and theologians of early Christianity. While serving (396-430) as bishop of Hippo Regius, the leading figure in the church, he was perhaps the greatest Christian thinker of all time and the one person with the biggest influence in theology for Catholics and Protestants, even more than the reformers. He also was the main person who influenced the "western world view," our cultural and identity both in Europe and the U.S.!

Augustine fought vigorously against his bad habits and sin nature, so he can grow deeper in our Lord. Until he learned a lesson from a small child, which he felt was the Word of God. Let Augustine's influence keep influencing you!

Lesson Outline:

Remember to begin in prayer!

- Prayer   5 min
- Pick one of the options   5-10 min
- Read lesson and bible passages   10-15min
- Discussion groups 15-30 min
- Going deep   5-10 min
- End in prayer and repeat application.   5 min

Total lesson time 45 min- 1 hr

Option:

Get several maps of your city {AAA is a great source}, preferably the large ones which you have trouble re-folding.

- Ask students to find various ways from their home to the church.
- Ask what is the shortest way?
- Have you ever went somewhere and got totally lost? Did you use a map?

Say: "Maps show us the big picture of streets and places of a city. They are designed to give directions, but do not actually give us the directions. We have to look at it and find our own way. Even though the directions are already there for us to see, we have to do the work to find them."

- How is this like the Bible?

We can just cruise along life without the effort to look in the map and see if we can find our way, but all we do is get ourselves lost, especially in an unknown big city: The city of life.

- Read Psalm 119:133

Option:

{Have students take turns reading this first section in a round, or highlight and assign readings to those who like to read in public.}

- The Bible calls us to faith and accountability in its entirety, to have faith in it without risk {since our place is already secured in heaven!}, and with trust in any situation we encounter.

- The Bible is reliable and stands the test of time, so is your trust there or elsewhere?

- The Bible is the reliable source of historical information, the record of God speaking!

- The Bible is the source for our contact and guidance with our creator!

- The Bible is our story, our history, our struggles, our opportunities, our hope, and the climax of His plan and redemption.

- The Bible tells who we are and what we are, it gives us purpose and meaning. Our response is how we choose to live.

- The Bible is our source for life, liberty, and happiness!

The Bible is not to be a secret, but shared and communicated with power and conviction, because it has been entrusted to us as bearers of, as agents of, and witness of it's truth!

- This will give you greater personal conviction! (Philippians 3:10)

- Your life will change! (John 1:1-3)

- Your attitudes will change! (I Cor. 5:10)

- You will be pointed in the right direction! {Isaiah 40:31}

- The glory of God will be pointed out to you! {Jeremiah 1:6f}

- The Bible will break through our self-will and deceptions, including sin, temptations, and rationalizations, because the Bible is the voice of God! {II Cor 11:1f}

- The temptation of Jesus was to satisfy His physical hunger, but His focus was the Father!

- There is no other final authority than the Word of God!

Lesson: "FIND OUT FOR YOURSELVES!!!"

REMEMBER: THE BIBLE CHANGES LIVES!!!

- You will become a greater person by being a greater servant.

- Your message and witness will be increased greatly.

- Bible study reveals real life principles for us all. Our problems and struggles become minor shadows to His glory!

The promise of scripture is that it may not promise us riches and problem free lives, what it does promise is His presence. When we place our trust in Christ because of His word to guide us, then we will have lives enriched with purpose, meaning, and fulfillment. Joshua 1:8; Proverbs 1; Psalm 1

- Let us not forget the results of placing Christ first in our lives! Psalm 119:11;105; John 8:31-36; 15:11; 16:33; 17:17

THE GOAL OF BIBLE STUDY: DON'T JUST INTERPRET IT, BUT APPLY TO YOUR LIFE!!!

REMEMBER: BE SURE TO INCORPORATE WHAT YOU KNOW INTO YOUR LIFE!!!

- It is not enough to know something; but we must be able to do something. This is what our response to grace and sanctification is about!

There are too many people in the world that just do not get it! Just as the Pharisees asked Jesus for a miracle after He fed over 4,000 people! Just as some crazy guy was screaming at the airport ticket person to get on his flight after they announced the airport is closed due to fog. Just as so many Christians sit in their pews every Sunday and do nothing for the Lord; they just do not get it! {Mark 8}

One of the great things about the Bible is it is honest with the characters that it portrays. If we were to write such a book, would we explain our weakness and stupidity, or how great we are? The Bible reveals the good, the bad, and the ugly, and it will with us too!

"You search the scriptures because you believe they give you eternal life. But the Scriptures point to me." {John 5:39 New Living Bible}

The question is do we get it? Since the Bible is God's authoritative Word, we no doubt will spend more time in it! Are we prepared to allow the Word of God to get in us, make changes, transform, and renew our minds for His glory? {Romans 12}

- If the Bible is not where you place your trust, then where is your trust and where will it lead you?

- We cannot have the Words of Jesus without the Bible.

NOW WHAT, NOW I KNOW WHY; WHAT DO I DO?

So how do we study the Bible? Countless copies of scripture are sold and sit on shelves and bookcases unread! Why? Because people do not know how to engage it, how to read the Word of our Lord: Too apprehensive with fear of conviction or unsure how to go about it.

Yet God himself gives us the directions and the ability to proceed. Matt 7:7John; 14:24; James 1:25

We can make the Bible real in our lives, so let us not be filled with fear or with apprehension; but put our discouragement away with confidence that we can go before God by the power of His Spirit, through His Word!

Discussion Questions:

This is the last study on the why and importance of the Bible.

Divide into your small groups and ask the group collectively to write a love letter to the Bible. They can also forego the small groups and do this individually, spending quite and alone time doing this.

In small groups or all together ask:

- What did you say and mean?

- What will you do now that you know you love the Bible?

- If you do not love the Bible why? What is in your way?

Application:

Turn off the lights and ask rhetorically: "What is passion?" "What are you passionate about?" Do you have passion for your Lord first, or yourself? If it is you, what is in the Lord's way?

"Going Deep:"

Spend time in prayer, pray that the Lord convicts everyone here with a passion and love for His Word.

Session VII

"Step I"

Teachers Study: "Thoughts on the Person and work of the Holy Spirit."

a) He is a person (John 14:16-17);

b) He is our advocate (John 14:16, I John 2:1);

c) He imparts new life (John 3:3-6);

d) He pleads our case before God the Father (Romans 8:26-27);

e) He bears witness and glorifies Christ (Romans 8:14, Galatians 4:6);

f) He pours God's love in our hearts (Romans 5:4-5, Galatians 5:22-23);

g) He is always with us (Matthew 28:20, Hebrews 13:5-6);

h) He indwells within us (John 14:17, Ephesians 3:16-17);

i) He is powerful and able to do the will of the Father through us (Acts 1:8, 4:31, 10:45);

j) He is essential for our salvation (John 3:5, I Corinthians 12:3);

k) He is essential for our sanctification (Romans 7:21-25, II Corinthians 3:18);

l) He is essential for our service and sharing of faith (Acts1:8);

m) He is Lord, loving, and available to us (I Corinthians 6:19-20);

It is our duty as Christians to recognize the role of the Holy Spirit, to find out our gifts that have been given. Then we must be discipled in those gifts and use our gifts to glorify His Kingdom. In doing this, we become obedient and we receive, rely, and trust in His role. (Acts 19:1-2, Romans 12:1-2, Galatians 5:13-26, Revelations 3:20, Ephesians 3:17, and Luke 11:13)

Lesson Outline:

Remember to begin in prayer!

- Prayer   5 min
- Pick one of the options   5-10 min
- Read lesson and bible passages   10-15min
- Discussion groups   15-30 min
- Going deep   5-10 min
- End in prayer and repeat application.   5 min

Total lesson time 45 min- 1 hr

"Options:"

First read the passage Galatians 2:20 and spontaneously create a "melodrama" or skit to illustrate it. Then have each group redo their skit or melodrama illustrating the opposite trait. For example first good attitude, then bad attitude. Our will for God, vs. our will for ourselves. Anticipate spending time with God vs. not; being alert for God vs. not! And so forth.

"Options:"

Get some marbles and scatter them on the floor, ask students to pick them up with their feet: first shoes on, then with shoes off, and finally with their hands.

- Ask, which was easier?

How is this like reading God's Word with knowing the right way of doing it?

Lesson: "Step I"

{After we have taken a hard look on the importance of the study of scripture, and what it means to us, now we can begin the process of "exegesis." Learn to draw out of the text, the meaning and intent and then transform and apply it to your life.}

STEP I: KNOWING THE KNOWABLE BRINGING OUR MIND TO BE RIGHT WITH GOD!

If you do not have the right attitude and mindset, you will not get much out of God's Word, because your will is in the way of His!

The Word of God will not allow us to stumble in the dark and be the straw that blows in the wind, dependent on the whims and trends of our culture. By knowing the knowable will keep us centered on what is right and true in a world that has lost its direction and compass. The world's relativism and materialism that has rejected truth and God will not capture us who place our trust in Christ. And our trust will gain momentum and growth through His Word.

Now that you have established a constant devotional time with God that includes Bible reading and prayer, you will find yourself hungering for More! That is the Holy Spirit working in you, desiring you to grow in Him! Desiring you to dive deeper and more earnestly into His Word.

FIRST: PRAYER!!! {Psalm 119:18} This is the essential first step to always, always start anything especially studying the Bible with communication to God!

- We must be in tune with the author to be able to understand His book!

SECOND: DIRECT YOUR WILL and seize the opportunity!!!

You have to make a commitment and stick to it. By sticking to it will allow you to become more motivated and constant, thus the more you do, the easier it becomes!

Make it a habit! Psychologists tell us it can take over 40 days for an action to become a habit. So be patient and invest the time, and do not expect instant results. Gifted mature Christians have spent decades studying it! So do not give up! Do not be like most people who give up after a few days or weeks!

- **Make a VOW, A Commitment.** Take the initiative! Be constant and continual, do not expect great grand slams off the first pitches, as with anything, it takes time!

- **You must have the desire.** {Mat 5:6}: *"Blessed are those who hunger and thirst after righteousness, for they shall be filled."*

- **Pick a Good Time.** {Mk 1:35} When you are the most alert and at your best. If you are not a night person then do not do it then! We need to give God the best part of our day, and not our leftovers! Sometimes it is best to split it in two, like morning and evening. **BE CONSISTENT!!!** Whatever the time, do not stand God up!

- **Remember the Morning Watch.** {Psalm 90:14} Most Christians through the centuries gave God that time! Because that is when we are usually most alert and uncluttered with the days activities.

If you start off halfheartedly you will fail!

You must allow the reading of the Word to be securely rooted in who you are as a person. Tell others what you are doing so they can hold you accountable!

THIRD: LOGGING TIME

- **Spend time** keeping the Bible Dusted. By reading and re-reading it!

- **Make a commitment** on how much you will read. Use a chart or a list to see your progress.

- **RELAX!** {Psalm 46:10} Quiet yourself and spend a little time Waiting on God, listening. Do not rush into God's Word! {PSALM 139:23-24} Do not be in a hurry, do not race through the Word of God! And do not bite off more than you can chew, reading more than you can.

SET GOALS FOR YOURSELVES.

- Make a commitment to how much time you will spend. I suggest starting off at 15 minutes after mastering the "7" minutes and then build up. Do not start with too much or you will burn out! Most mature Christians spend over 1 hour a day. 15 minutes in the morning, 15 minutes at lunch and 15 minutes before bed will = 45 minutes. {You have 168 hours in a week, how much will belong to God?}

- Make a commitment when you will read; For example: Start off in the morning and then again in the evening, and slowly start to increase the time. Do not watch the clock, stay focused!

REMEMBER: Quality is more important then Quantity!

- **Have a Special Place.** Have a place you can go constantly that has few distractions and is comfortable with good lighting and secluded. {Gen. 19:27, Luke 22:39} Be alone, where it is quiet and you will not be disturbed, where you can pray out loud too.

- Watch your life change as the glory of our Lord Jesus Christ works out in your life (Philippians 2:1-18).

- Then, Pray, and pray again!

FOURTH: BE OPEN TO THE HOLY SPIRIT

- Unless you are open to Him, how can he teach you? {John 16:13}

- **John 1:9:** *"The true light that gives light to every one was coming into the world."*

- Do not go into Bible Study with your own agenda; rather let the Holy Spirit direct you.

- Always use discernment and guidance from experienced Bible students!

- Rely on the Power of God!

God's Word is knowable to us! As clear as crystal, in fact more clear than anything ever written in religion or philosophy; clearer than your daily newspaper!

ALWAYS: BEGIN and END YOUR STUDY IN PRAYER.

Ask the Lord to open your eyes for guidance, insight and application; open your heart to His Will. {II Tim 2:15}

Discussion Questions:

1. What are you thankful for in life?

2. What do you take for granted?

3. How have you studied scripture in the past?

4. Have you ever put a significant effort into prayer before you read?

5. Why do we tend not to?

6. If it is so important, why do we not put in the effort in the things that are the most important, such as relationships, Bible, devotions, etc. it seems the most important aspects of life are the ones we spend the least effort?

7. So do you take the Bible for granted with its abundance and availability? Some people in closed countries like China would literally cut off a hand to get a copy of God's Word?

8. How does it make you feel that some people truly desire to study and know God's Word, but have no access to it?

9. What can you do to have a thirst and desire to know God's Word?

10. Why do people fail to be consistent in their devotions?

11. Have you ever thought much in the role of the Holy Sprit in your life?

12. How can you rely on the Holy Sprit?

13. If God's Word is so clear, then why are there so many interpretations out there? And why do people, including Christians, not take it seriously?

14. What are the steps you can do to develop a consistent Spirit filled and joyful time of Bible reading and devotions?

15. Are you willing to make a commitment and stick to it, to put in the effort so it is a joy and not a chore? How?

"Q & A:"

Spend a few minutes answering group questions and asking what did they learn in the small groups?

"Application:" Pick one of the following:

A. Have students write a letter of commitment to themselves to:

1. Pick a time, and place to read the Bible as devotion.

2. Pick a book of the Bible and commit to studying it within 6 months.

   Collect the letters and give them back after 6 months.

B. Give a copy of a chapter from the Bible, such as I Cor. 13, and have the students practice "getting the right mindset."

"Going Deep:" Close in a song or hymn with the lights out.

SESSION VIII

Step II

Teachers Study: "Looking beyond Ourselves"

There are times when I journal, that is keep a diary of what is going on in my life. I sometimes look back on them and gain new insight on what I was going through, that I did not have back then. I have become more adept to interpret God's leading and plan for me the more I experience life and receive what He has done. By looking back on what we have been through and see the hand of God there, it will give great comfort and encouragement for what lies ahead or what we are going through now.

As I gain new insight into my personality and the Lord's working into my issues and problems, I realize how shadows they are compared to my Lord's holiness and greatness.

By concentrating on Christ and what He has done will lift us up better and more complete than anything we could ever do. Thus the thrust of journaling has taught me is to look beyond myself and keep focused on Christ. The other end of journaling is a problem that people, including Christians, in their zeal keep faithful to their journals, is that they become self absorbed and only see themselves and their problems and not the Lord. So be careful if you do this exercise of journaling, keep focused on why you are doing it, that is to grow closer to the Lord and not to yourself.

We are called to keep focused on Him and not ourselves, so we are looking at God's Word as a mirror to ourselves, to our soul, as not to see us, but to see God working in us. When we only see ourselves, we see sin, brokenness, failure, self-seeking inclinations, and wrong attitudes.

We must see God's interests and not our own, then the journey of maturing in the faith will become more real as our problems become less, He becomes more.

The same thing can happen when we read the Word. We become so consumed with our interests, we do not see the calling and response we are to give. Thus we grow bitter, thinking that this devotion stuff is not for me, so we turn it off. We replace it with so much activity that God is pushed out of our lives, except on Sunday morning. But even then we are rushed and stressed and do not feel the worship or hear the lesson. We only hear ourselves, our problems of getting the kids ready, or the stress at work or at school. The results of a mature life will respond from the impact of our devotional life, by applying what Christ has done.

We need to respond to the text with a surrendered will and a mind cleared of our anxious thoughts. When we are focused on our fears, hopes, dreams, needs, or emotions, we have no room to learn what God has for us. We will not be able to think deeply enough into the text so there is a transformation of our nature and will, as philosophers call our existential core. There can be no serious behavior or personality change unless the core of who we are changes. And Christ is the only one who does that right!

This transformation in Romans 12 cannot happen when we are in the way. God does as He pleases, but He usually does not override our will. He waits for us to be surrendered and poured out to Him. So do not take the chance and allow your stubbornness to get in the way of God working in you!

Lesson Outline:

Remember to begin in prayer!

- Prayer   5 min
- Pick one of the options   5-10 min
- Read lesson and bible passages   10-15min {you can do this and discussions together}
- Discussion groups   15-30 min
- Going deep   5-10 min
- End in prayer and repeat application.   5 min

Total lesson time 45 min- 1 hr

"Options:"

Get some marbles and scatter them on the floor, ask students to pick them up with their feet: first shoes on, then with shoes off, and finally with their hands.

- Ask, which was easier?

How is this like reading God's Word with knowing the right way of doing it?

"Options:"

- Ask, "If you were on a long trip, What could you can hardly wait to get back to? Your bed, friends, boyfriend/ girl friend/ husband/ wife, hobby, TV, computer, Bible, school, car, shower, your room, video games, parents, work, music, church, or pets?"

- Ask, "what gives you peace and joy?

- Do the two questions have the same answer?

- If so why? If not, why?

- You can show a movie clip of "The Wizard of Oz" where Dorothy says, "there is no place like home."

- Home is where we find comfort and safety, is God your home?

- Read Psalm 84

Lesson: Step II "HOW:" THE METHOD OF GETTING INTO GOD'S WORD

{For this lesson use a computer software program and print off a chapter of Scripture. Romans 12 is a good one to start with, lots of stuff to dig into. You can give a quick overview of this and then jump into the discussion.}

These are the basics on how we can go about studying God's Word. This is called the science of "exegetical method," but there is no need for big words here. These are the basic procedures a pastor or experienced teacher of the Word will learn in Bible School and Seminary to prepare sermons and commentaries. But boiled down in a clearer and simpler way for you to understand and apply.

This will allow you to better understand and apply God's Word and then even teach it to others! These methods are not for the professional Christians only, they are the tools for all disciples of the Lord!

Remember there is no "best way," only that we do it. This study is about placing the "bur" under the saddle to get the horse moving or plugging in the computer so we can use it!

REMEMBER: It is simply not enough to know what you want to do. You have to know the right way of doing it. Like following a recipe in cooking or working on your car with the manual.

FIRST: PRAY! {Proverbs 2:4}

- Ask God into your study as your teacher. Ask Him to free your mind from distractions and help you concentrate. You are entering a learning partnership with Christ!

- A good plan is essential to any undertaking.

SECOND: LOOK AT THE WHOLE BOOK (i.e. a single book in the Bible)

For example; if you are going to study John, read the book of John in an easy to read translation, like the "New Living Translation." Read it like reading a favorite novel! Enjoy it! Read it through in one sitting with no distractions. An average reader will take 30 minutes to 1 hour. That way you will gain an overall understanding. It is best to do this step two or three times!

- Preview it. Read it like a novel, try the New Living Bible. Then Read slowly and keep re-reading, this will help you remember.

- Like a wide-angle lens, "OVERVIEW" the big picture. Remember the context! See the whole picture of what is going on. The reason most people do not get it is because they do not get in it!

- Study whole books; book by book and not just topics.

- Like putting together a puzzle, start with a corner and then the straight edges. Start with the obvious in its context, and the rest will be revealed from there!

THIRD: READ CAREFULLY. EXAMINE IT WITH A MICROSCOPE.

"WHOLE TO PARTS TO WHOLE"

- Start by skimming, then re-read more carefully, then read it very carefully and slowly. Then check out commentaries and dictionaries. Repetition is the key to understanding!

- Read carefully; study it! Use the NIV or NASB versions. Do not be distracted and do not stop. Try reading aloud for better concentration.

- Do not read a passage here and there. Read through a whole book through and through systematically, you are not at a buffet.

- Imagine yourself as a participant. As if it is your story. As if you are there.

- Let God speak to you, as the main goal is to know our Lord better, not just to gain more knowledge!

- Look out for topics, logic and direction.

- Meditate and pray over the passages that "Speak" to you as you re-read, then memorize those key passages.

FOURTH: MAKE USE OF THE BOOK CHART.

Write down what God is saying to you and what you have discovered and learned. Doing this will allow you to apply it to your life better!

- Examine what is being said.

> I.   In chapters.
> II. In Paragraphs
> III. In Verses.

ALWAYS BE AWARE OF THE CONTEXT!!!

See it!!!
Know it!!!
Do it!!!

REMEMBER: BIBLE STUDY IS WORK!!!

Growing in the spirit is a day by day growth; just like learning to read, the study of mathematics, science, or playing a musical instrument. It takes time and effort!

HARD WORK WILL PAY OFF!

"Discussion Questions:"

Take your passage, {Rom. 12 or choose a short book like II or III John or Jude or...} and go through it together or in small groups with these steps.

1. PRAY! {Proverbs 2:4}

- Ask God into your study as your teacher.

2. SECOND: LOOK AT THE WHOLE BOOK {for this lesson chapter, or chose a shout book like II or III John or Jude or…}

- Preview it in a paraphrase. OVERVIEW

3. THIRD: READ CAREFULLY WHOLE TO PARTS TO WHOLE

- Start by skimming, then re-read more carefully, then read it very carefully and slowly.

- Then read carefully; study it! Use the NIV or NASB versions.

- Q:" How can we imagine ourselves as a participant, as if it is our story, as if we are there?"

- Remember to let God speak to you, "Meditate," as the main goal is to know our Lord better, not just to gain more knowledge!

- Look for topics, logic, and direction.

4. FOURTH: MAKE USE OF THE BOOK CHART. Or just use a separate sheet of paper to write down what you have discovered and learned.

- Examine what is being said.

I.   In chapters.
II. In Paragraphs
III. In Verses.

"Application:"

Ask the students to try to keep a journal or diary of their devotional reading this week. At least a list of what they read and when they read it.

"Going Deep:"

Ask students to find a secluded and quiet place, and spend that time with God for the remaining of the time. They can also go over with God what they learned.

SESSION IX

"Step III"

Teachers Study: "The Importance of Theology"

The problem we have today is most people, including Christians, do not know the reasons and importance of theology, including the role of scripture. People cannot discern when or how God works, what He has to tell us or what we should know until he tells us. The Lord tells us who He is and reveals His will to us through the authority of His word. John 5:39 and II Timothy 3:16. These scriptures testify to the importance and role and authority of the Bible, that the Bible is the supreme authority of faith, practice, and duty for all Christians. There is no higher authority either ecclesiastical or personal that can take the place of God's word. A conservative, strong position on biblical inspiration is imperative to the effective Bible teacher. Without this view of authority, we elevate ourselves above God and we become the means of faith and practice and not the Creator of the universe. The Bible is "wholly true." This is testified by the scriptures themselves, by the test of time, and even by science and higher criticism. Without the authority of scripture is like having a view of Christianity without Christ.

Lesson Outline:

Remember to begin in prayer!

- Prayer   5 min
- Pick one of the options   5-10 min
- Read lesson and bible passages   10-15min {you can do this and discussions together}
- Discussion groups   15-30 min
- Going deep   5-10 min
- End in prayer and repeat application.   5 min

Total lesson time 45 min- 1 hr

"Options"

Go over the following: Read John 3:16. {You can have youth say this in a round as loud as they can}

Group One say:	Group Two say:
God	"the greatest giver"
so loved	"the greatest motive"
the world	"the greatest need"
that he gave	"the greatest act"
His only son	"the greatest gift"
that whosoever	"the greatest invitation"
believes in Him	"the greatest opportunity"
should not perish	"the greatest deliverance"
but have eternal life.	"the greatest joy"

"Options"

Get a hold of several dirty filters, such as from an auto repair shop or an old furnace filter. And get a clean filter, preferably one you can see through, such as a "glass" gas filter.

You can do the same with various types of magazines, from teen magazines, to Christianity Today…

Say: "A filter screens out what is bad and harmful. The filter to your air conditioner and heater at home filters out dust that many people are allergic to. These auto filters screen out contaminates so the car will get better gas mileage and last longer."

I once saw a car that was never tuned up or had any oil changes, in fact it had the original oil in it, which was sludge! The car was totally worthless. It was a two year old Lincoln Continental with only 30,000 miles on it! But the engine, transmission and many of the car's systems did not work. The car should have sold for over $20,000 and still be an almost new car! But this car ended up at an auction and sold for $2000 as scrap! When we do not filter out contaminates, we too can become scrap!

- We have to learn how to screen out what is false from what is true!

- Read Phil. 1:9-11; 4:8-9

- What are some of the contaminates in your life?

- What can you do to filter them?

- What would your life be with a good filter?

Lesson: Step III "OBSERVE IT."{II TIM 2:15} ASK WHAT DOES IT SAY?

Now Begin a detailed study of the passage. You thought you already did? Actually you have just begun! Now Begin a detailed study of the passage and write down what you see in the chart on "Step IV" or in a notebook or diary.

- Effective observation takes time and practice. So be patient.

Observation is taking a careful look of what is going on. And we have to know what is going on before we can act on a plan or action. A good police officer must know the situation before they can intercede correctly. Bible students must know the Word themselves before they can teach it.

Too many people like to dive into a decision without looking at the options and consequences. Too many Bible students will jump into teaching without fully knowing their subject, that is why we have so much bad teaching on TV, and so many false teachings and blatant heresies in the church.

Emotions and desires have been substituted for principle logic and study, greed and power have replaced honoring our Lord!

Like planning a road trip, you need to know where you are going; and then you can look back where you have been: Get Ready to CHART IT! That is to write down what you learn, so you can go back to it and see how you have grown and to review His incredible Word! This will be step VII.

OBSERVING IS: Before the process of interpretation, ask, "**What does it say?**" You must do this before you ask what does it mean and how to apply it to your life!

- If you do the opposite as many do, you will **not** go deep enough and allow God's Word to transform you before you respond to that change!

- When we try to do something for God before we are changed, it is like trying to drive a car manual instead of the car itself: When we are working with the plans only and not the finished product, we will end up accomplishing nothing!

Discussion HOW TO DO THE OBSERVATION:

[Take your passage, {chose a short book like II or III John or Jude or...} and go through it together or in small groups with these steps. Have the students highlight or circle what they find. It is best to give them several different colors of highlighters, and use different colors for different observations.]

1. Give the Book the "Looks."

- **Look** for a stated purpose.

- **Look** for repeated phrases.

- **Look** for the point.

- **Look** who is involved?

If you do not know what to "look" for, you will not find much!

2. **Look** for the time of events, the sequence, "once, then, now, will be, etc." Once you know what to look for a whole new world opens up to

you! You will see the words come to you as marvelous revelations as the Holy Spirit comes upon you!

- **Look** for persons, places, event, and ideas.

3. Look for logical Connectives, i.e. Therefore, But, Since, So, Thus, Because, For, That, etc. (Conjunction junction what's your function?) This is very important because it tells us of a transition, summary or application from a logic statement or line of reasoning.

Such as:

- BUT, Even though, Much More, Yet, Although, Then, and Nevertheless is a **"Contrast,"** the ideas and information that point to a difference, that set themselves off from each other for comparison and emphasis.

- As, For, and So, refers to a **"Correlative,"** that is a mutual dependency, a pair that is closely related to each other.

- Until, Now, When, Before, After, Since, Where and While are time or place references and, in grammar, called **"Temporal Connectors."** They refer to a time and/or place. Use a Bible map to see for yourself.

- Because, For this reason, For…, and Since refer to a **"Reasoning."** They draw conclusions and inferences from the argument and/or information presented. They include causes, motives, justifications, explanations, ideas, acts, sense, and conclusions that result to name a few.

- Too, Also, As, Just, Likewise, And, So Also, and Like are "**Comparisons.**" They communicate parallel ideas and facts that are similar or different.

- So Then, Therefore, As a result, Thus, and Then are **Results.** Usually a consequence, issue or effect that has or will happen. Or a boiling down of the point for an application, the Epistles are filled with them. See a "therefore," then ask what is it there for?

- That, So That, and In Order That, are also "**results**" but with more of a specific Purpose.

- IF is a **Condition** flowing from a logical argument. It usually starts off with IF and concludes a meaning with THEN. That the truth depends on the preceding statement or requirement and "If" is the "sound bite" referring to a conclusion that has a condition attached. "Then" is the consequence or conclusion of the argument. "If you touch a hot stove, **then** you will get burned."

Notice other important words!

REMEMBER: VERY EXTREMELY IMPORTANT IS THE CONTEXT!!!

The context is what is going on around the passage you are studying. If you take and read one verse without carefully studying the previous and preceding text, you will miss a great deal and possibly misinterpret what is being said. Some of the preachers on TV love to do this, that is why so many people are being led astray by false teaching!!!

4. THINGS TO OBSERVE:

- **Verbs are crucial!** If you are not sure of the meaning then check "Webster's." But beware the verb meanings are in English and may not correspond to the original meaning {That is why we check several translations}. Check **NOUNS** in "Bible Dictionaries." The context will give you the clues!

- Define the meaning of the important words you are studying. Do not assume you know. Check it out, by looking them up!

- Notice the setting.

- Consider words used more than once, and repeated phrases.

- Compare passages/verses to similar verses i.e. "Scripture interprets scripture." Use a concordance or a "Chain Reference Bible."

- Notice the implications

- Notice what is being taught

- Notice the promises

- Notice carefully the underlining principle[s]

- What about the life, work, teaching, presence of Jesus Christ?

- Look out for types of "literary style." That is history, philosophy, drama, poetry, wisdom and law. The Bible is a collection of 66 books written over a 1,500 year period of time, each with its own literary style. Some books are "history" such as I & II Kings and I & II

Chronicles. Some books are "Law" such as Leviticus and Deuteronomy. See appendix A

- Look at different translations {at least 3, such as NIV, NASB, and a paraphrase like CEV, NLT, or the "Amplified Bible." Get a "Parallel Bible," it has several translations side by side. Like looking at a diamond from only one angle is like looking at glass, you see nothing interesting or spectacular. But when you turn the diamond in the light you see all the facets and depth, so it is with scripture! Looking at various translations side by side is like looking at more facets, it brings out the "3-D" depth, and becomes clearer and easier to understand and then to teach!

"Application": {chose one}

A. Have students practice making an **"emotional identification"** into the text. That is to place yourself as a participant being active in it, as if it is your story, as if you are there. We do this naturally when we watch a good movie or TV show. We become a participant vicariously. It captures our attention and interest, as if we are there! Thus we will cry or laugh, because it touched us.

- How do you do this when you see a really good movie or TV show?

- How can you do this with Scripture?

Nothing is more interesting or spectacular than the stories in the Bible, so what is stopping you from being active in it?

B. Have students look up some of the verbs they found in a dictionary and compare the meanings to a "word study" book. You can borrow one from your pastor.

- What is the difference and similar meanings?

- How can we be sure what we read is what we read?

"Digging Deeper:"

Have the students spend five minutes praying for 5 people that are not relatives. Have them do this separately and as far away from each other as possible.

SESSION X

"STEP III (B)"

Teachers Study: "Doing the Word"

—Chuck Swindoll says in his book, "Improving Your Serve:"

"To make the value of obedience just as practical as possible, let's play 'Let's Pretend.' Let's pretend that you work for me. In fact, you are my executive assistant in a company that is growing rapidly. I'm the owner and I'm interested in expanding overseas. To pull this off, I make plans to travel abroad and stay there until a new branch office gets established. I make all the arrangements to take my family and move to Europe for six to eight months. And I leave you in charge of the busy stateside organization. I tell you that I will write you regularly and give you directions and instructions. I leave and you stay.

Months pass. A flow of letters are mailed from Europe and received by you at the national headquarters. I spell out all my expectations.

Finally, I return. Soon after my arrival, I drive down to the office and I am stunned. Grass and weeds have grown up high. A few windows along the street are broken. I walk into the receptionist's room and she is doing her nails, chewing gum, and listening to her favorite disco station {as you can see the book was written in the 70's}. I look around and notice the wastebaskets are overflowing.

181

The carpet hasn't been vacuumed for weeks, and nobody seems concerned that the owner has returned. I asked about your whereabouts and someone in the crowded lounge area points down the hall and yells, "I think he's down there." Disturbed, I move in that direction and bump into you as you are finishing a chess game with our sales manager. I ask you to step into my office, which has been temporarily turned into a television room for watching afternoon soap operas.

"What in the world is going on, man?"

"What do you mean, Chuck?"

"Well, look at this place! Didn't you get any of my letters?"

"Letters? Oh yes! Sure! I got every one of them. As a matter of fact, Chuck, we have had a letter study every Friday night since you left. We have even divided the personnel into small groups to discuss many of the things you wrote. Some of the things were really interesting. You will be pleased to know that a few of us have actually committed to memory some of your sentences and paragraphs. One or two memorized an entire letter or two – Great stuff in those letters."

"Okay, you got my letters. You studied them, meditated on them, discussed them, and even memorized them. But what did you do about them?"

"Do? We didn't do anything about them."

Lesson Outline:

Remember to begin in prayer!

- Prayer   5 min
- Pick one of the options   5-10 min
- Read lesson and bible passages   10-15min {you can do this and discussions together}
- Discussion groups   15-30 min

- Going deep   5-10 min
- End in prayer and repeat application.   5 min

Total lesson time 45 min- 1 hr

"Options:"

Get a hold of some traffic signs. You can borrow them from the DMV {ask for the safety division if in CA} or a school drivers ed., you can make your own, or have a Sunday school class make them. You need a stop sign, yield, and any others.

Say: "What is this sign for {stop}?," Read Ex. 20:14 and ask, "How is this verse like a stop sign?"

Say: "What is this sign for {Yield}?" Read Rom. 14:13 and ask, "How is this verse like the yield sign?"

"Options:"

Ask your students to choose one of the following statements that best applies to their life now {you can type them up on cards for them or use in small groups}:

1. I'm moving away from God.

2. I'm stagnant in my faith.

3. I'm growing, but very slowly.

4. I'm growing.

5. I'm on fire; I grow every day.

6. One area where I really need to grow is:

Lesson: STEP III (B): OBSERVE IT. ASK WHAT DOES IT MEAN?

When observing, we first ask what it says, then and only then can we observe what it means. Too many people like to get into a hurry and "cut to the chase" for the meaning, and miss a lot and even get the meaning wrong! This is the crucial step we have to undertake before we apply it to our lives. There are no easy ways out, or shortcuts to understanding any great works of literature, especially God's Word!

This is the task called "exegesis." This fancy word simply means to study a text carefully, logically and systematically, to find the original intended meaning.

This is the process of gaining the "plain truth" of what the passage you are studying means. It is more than just "common sense," and it is common sense. This is where we pick at the text and in so doing we are picking at our hearts and minds!

Remember we must come before the Word with an open heart and mind. This will allow us to discover more of the meaning. We cannot be closed off to His work, and what He has to teach us. We cannot have our own agenda and expectations that take up all the room in our hearts and minds, that leave no room for God. We cannot have a mind already made up in our image and limited experience. God is fully capable, but He does not usually steam roll over our will. He allows us to work it out, that is what Philippians 2 is all about.

- If we go to scripture to only be comforted, we will find ourselves spiritually bankrupted.

"I have been crucified with Christ and I no longer live, but Christ lives in me. The life I live in the body, I live by faith in the Son of God, who loved me and gave himself for me." {Gal. 2:20}

We must go before our Lord with the attitude of being poured out before Him with nothing left of our will. Then humbly ask, "please my Lord reveal to me what you want me to learn and to grow. Reveal to me the things you wish me to change, show me how I can be my best for your glory."

- When we go before God with only what we want, all we will hear in return is our echoed assumptions!

"You have seen many things, but have paid no attention; your ears are open, but you hear nothing." {Isaiah 42:20}

We will not gain much with the attitude to just ask God to show us a neat trick, or just help me through this issue, or to just bless me… We must have a lifestyle of conviction and learning. Even when the revelation may shake us out of our tree of comfort. Everything God has to reveal to us is wonderful, however we may not see the wonder until years latter, or not even until we are called home.

Take comfort that God is sovereign. He is in charge. And He does have a wonderful plan for you. Just beware we cannot go through the committed life of a disciple with the fear of being convicted, or hide in the face of challenge. We cannot tremble as ostriches with our heads in the sand, ignoring the truth that the Holy Spirit has for us. We must be prepared to receive conviction and be willing to change. We need to have an open door to being disturbed. Thus, instead of the "do not disturb" sign on the door to our Lord, it must say "come on in, disturb all you want." Because God is God and we are not!

- Let God have His way with you!

- We must know our weakness and limitations as creatures filled with sin!

- Ask our Lord to open you before Him, to allow yourself to go beyond your culture, education and experience! Then the meaning will come alive!

- We cannot apply what we do not know and understand!

Watch God's Word unfold before you.

When you read, ask yourself "What does it mean?"

- Look for meanings of words and phrases in the context! Use Bible Dictionaries.

- Look at different translations side by side. I Recommend the N.I.V. or N.A.S.B. for serious study, but the New Living Bible, J.B. Philips, The Message, Amplified, C.E.V., and New Century versions make good insights. Remember they are paraphrases and not accurate translations. Do not take them literally. Just allow them to give you insight. And overview.

- ANALYZE by gathering facts and all the information available to you.

Do not solely rely on commentaries and study Bibles. Nothing beats studying for yourself. You will get addicted to relying on them and get lazy on your personal studies! Use the commentaries just to see what you may have missed, and what you do not understand!

THINGS TO DO:

- Paraphrase the passage yourself.

- What is supported?

- What are the conclusions?

- **REMEMBER:** Be on the look out for **VERBS.** They are crucial. "Tense, voice, person, & mood." You know the stuff from grade school! If you need help, check out a grammar textbook. Some dictionaries have basic English summaries that will be a great help! Keep in mind the Bible was not written in English! For more serious study, check out "Colin-Brown" by Regency, which goes through the Greek words and gives in-depth insights.

The BIG THING TO DO:

Make an emotional identification into the text. Place yourself as a participant, being active in it. **As if it is your story. As if you are there.** We do this naturally when we watch a good movie or TV show. We become a participant vicariously. It captures our attention and interest, as if we are there! Thus we will cry or laugh, because it touched us. Nothing is more interesting or spectacular than the stories in the Bible, so what is stopping you from being active in it?

"Discussion:" THINGS TO VIEW AND ASK AND TO APPLY:

Take your passage, {choose a short book like II or III John or Jude or...} and go through it together or in small groups with these steps.

Ask what is actually being said? Consider nothing insignificant!

- Look for stuff to carry out in your life.

- Write down your questions and what you do not understand. This helps us grow!!!

- What are the implications to be applied?

- What is being taught to transform us?

- What are the promises that I can take to heart?

- What about the life, work, teaching, and presence of Jesus Christ, how can I model His Character?

- What is our duty?

- What is God's character?

- Look out for types of "literary style." That is history, philosophy, drama, poetry, wisdom and law. {See appendix A}

- Make a commitment to the meaning.

- Try to write the verse or entire passage in your own words!

- Accept what It says: **This is God's Word!**

"Application:"

Use these observations to be more focused in your life. Notice the duty or application from your text, and commit to it!

"Going Deep:"

Read the following article by candlelight, you may remember it from the teacher's study:

If someone said the word *"holiness"* to you, what would come to your mind first? You'd probably associate holiness with God. But did you ever stop to think about what God's holiness is all about?

What does the Bible mean when it says, *"Holy, holy, holy is the LORD Almighty"* (Isaiah 6:3)?

The word "holy" is translated in from the Old Testament and it means, "separated" or "cut apart." God is holy because He is totally, completely, absolutely separate from everything He has ever created. Because He cannot be infected by sin! He is a cut above everything in the universe.

He is perfect, pure, and separate from the slightest hint of sin, error or evil. Can you visualize perfection in your life, that is living out a totally perfect sinless existence? It is not easy, is it? What about purity, that's just as difficult. Have you ever wondered how we are to understand God's holiness if we can't picture what it means?

Well God provided a Way for us to understand Him, a model for us to follow. Jesus said, *"Anyone who has seen me has seen the Father"* (John 14:9). If we want to "see" the holiness of God more clearly, we need to look at the life Jesus Christ. Jesus was holy in that He was perfect. He never made a mistake. He never miscalculated or judged incorrectly. He always did the right thing at the right time in the right way

Jesus was holy in that He was and is pure. He never sinned (can you imagine that?). Yes, He walked among sinners. He mingled with them, ate with them, laughed with them, cried with them, healed them, and loved them. But He never became attached to their sinful attitudes or actions. And, with love and care, He called them to leave their lives of sin (John 8:11). God is like that.

But that's not all. Our holy God Expects us to be holy too: *"But just as he who called you is holy, so be holy in all you do; for it is written: Be holy, because I am holy."* (1 Peter 1:15-16)

Now we can say this is a tough standard, but does this mean we do not try because it is so tough? Thus if we will never reach it, why bother with it. A lot of Christians live their lives this way. So they never try, but we must try anyway. We can get closer to God's standard of holiness every day by relinquishing ourselves to Christ in our prayers, devotions, and relationships. And we can rejoice in the fact that a day is coming when we will stand in God's presence as holy people singing *"Holy, holy, holy is the LORD Almighty!!!"*

So let us go out and live as our life belongs to our Lord, as it does, and be holy!

SESSION XI

"The importance of context and tools"

Teachers Study: "Blame SHIFTING"

"The man said, The woman you put here with me—she gave me some fruit from the tree, and I ate it. Then the LORD God said to the woman, What is this you have done? The woman said, The serpent deceived me, and I ate." {Gen. 3:12-13}

As soon as man sinned, he quickly commenced to blame others. One of the effects of sin is the refusal to take responsibility for our actions. This is the attitude, which is so popular today from young people to Presidents. This is the favorite manner in which most people handle guilt, which is they blame others. They do this for two reasons:

- First; they do not want to live with guilt.

- Second: they do not want to suffer the consequences of their actions.

Blaming others allows an escape mechanism, like an ejection seat that avoids the consequences {crash = suffering} by bailing out. However, this is not as effective as most people think. Freeing the burden of guilt by escaping only puts it off until later, while in the meantime it grows and spreads out of control, and continues to gnaw away at our conscience. So this defense mechanism only makes matters worse. "Blame Shifting" can be illustrated by visualizing an old fashioned scale. As one side of the scale becomes increasingly loaded with the weight of guilt, the guilt ridden person just shifts the guilt to the other side of the scale. And we all do this by blaming others.

There is just one problem with this {okay a lot more problems}, the act of blaming others instead of taking the responsibility for one's own actions flies in the face of the Gospel. It is unjust and serves only to increase the guilt and the problems we incur with others in our relationships. This becomes a pattern of dysfunctional behavior that is an endless loop of a hopeless cycle.

In spite of Adam and Eve's "Clinton-isk" slick blame shifting, God held them accountable and they suffered the consequences of their disobedience.

"To Adam he said, Because you listened to your wife and ate from the tree about which I commanded you, You must not eat of it, Cursed is the ground because of you." {Gen. 3:17}

God not only held him responsible for his action, He also held him responsible for listening to the voice of his wife {the influence of others!!!} instead of listening to the voice of God. His excuse only served to increase his personal responsibility and guilt. We must learn that God does not allow us to avoid the consequences of our actions by blaming others. In fact we are held responsible for blaming others. We may think we can get away with it as certain presidents have, but make no mistake, if we fail to hold each other accountable for our actions, you can be sure that God will hold us responsible.

"So then, each of us will give an account of himself to God. Therefore let us stop passing judgment on one another. Instead, make up your mind not to put any stumbling block or obstacle in your brother's way." {Romans 14:12-13}

On the day of judgment, there will be no opportunities for blame shifting. Those who have cleverly "Clintonized" the laws of God will one day discover that God and His Law are inflexible.

Lesson Outline:

Remember to begin in prayer!

- Prayer   5 min
- Only one "Open" option   5-10 min
- Read lesson and bible passages   10-15min {you can do this and discussions together}
- Discussion groups   15-30 min
- Going deep   5-10 min
- End in prayer and repeat application.   5 min

Total lesson time 45 min- 1 hr

"Open"

Gather together some different kinds of underwear for display purposes {preferably clean}, and say; "several years ago there was a commercial on TV where a man in an elevator announced he was "feeling good all over" as he was dancing around. And the then the announcer says, "Hanes makes you feel good all under."

- What is your favorite kind of underwear?

- Have you ever felt so excited about something that you wanted to announce it to the world?

- We may not report how much we like our underwear, but what do you report with excitement to your friends?

Read Proverbs 19: 21-23

Ask, what do you think when someone is more concerned how they feel and think over against the truth?

- Can you think of an example?

- Is it okay to feel and think wrong as long as you feel it is okay?

- Is God more concerned with truth or feelings?

- Is it tough remaining in integrity at your school or work?

Read I John 2:15-17

- How does this thinking effect the way we interpret Scripture?

Lesson: "The importance of context and tools"

So why do Christians disagree on a lot of points?

First we may make a lot of "LOGICAL" errors, and misinterpret it, take a passage[s] out of its context, or rush through it. We look at one ambiguous text and ignore the clear scores of others. Christians are not perfect and are subject to reasoning and judgment fallacies. Even the greatest scientific minds disagree for these same reasons! Hence why there are so many theories in science, and they are always changing.

Second, we are **limited by the education and knowledge** we process, and by the information at our disposal, and knowing how to use that information! Our perspectives are limited and we do not always see the big picture, thus our interpretations are sometimes flawed, or adequate work and effort were not put into it.

Third, One of the biggest causes of errors is **our prejudice.** That is our preconceived ideas and biases that cloud our thinking. Such as believing in a particular mode of baptism. We may grow up in a church that practices "believers baptism" or "infant baptism" only, thus are unwilling to look deeper theologically at the other views.

People tend to rationalize their faulty beliefs instead of researching and discovering the facts for themselves. Or they do not want to know or grow beyond their limited experience, or base decisions on emotions and do not seriously see the logic.

Fourth, we are still **full of sin** and fall way short, thus we are susceptible to the influences of Satan and are unable to reason with true perfection!

For example in John 1:1, the Jehovah's Witnesses believe Jesus is not God, but "a god" as Lucifer to is "a god" in their theology. In I Corinthians 15:29 the Mormons believe it is okay to baptize people who have already died. In Mark 16:18, some American Appalachian sects handle poisonous snakes to prove their faith. Some Bible teachers on TV use III John 2 as an excuse to teach the "health and wealth" gospel. Yet when you examine these texts they do not teach any of those things! These are classic cases of bad interpretation for the reasons fore mentioned.

- **The Bible does not teach anything we please.**

- **The Bible cannot mean something else from what it does say. The Bible cannot mean what it never meant!**

These are three crucial areas of "exegesis" that we have to know before we can interpret correctly:

1. **We must be aware of our nature,** that is we as fallen humans will compare all that we see hear, read and understand to what we have already previously experienced and have learned. We also have to take into account our culture, education, emotional level, and anything else that makes us human and separated from the pure character of God. Thus we are extremely limited in our scope to perceive in a pure logical and precise way {hence why people disagree on every subject known}.

2. **We must be aware of the nature of Scripture** and the Divine Authors intent. There are several different types of literature or as scholars say "genre" {pronounced jon-ra} types, by different human writers with different cultures, education and audience, all Divinely inspired.

3. In the same thought, God has given us a very capable brain and resources to use. In other words "you can do it."

Thus we are the interpreters! What we read all filters through our will and perceptions and then we try to make sense of it. It also filters through the types of literature, the "dual nature" of Scripture, which is the Divine Author and the human hand that penned it {God's Word is still infallible and inspired through this dual nature}. We cannot just infuse our experience and limited understanding into the text what is not there and give the credit to the Holy Spirit. We cannot think that our way of thinking is the correct and only way {hence why there are so many denominations}. Because even the meaning and expression of a word can vary from person to person as we add our perceptions into everything.

- The Bible was written by the words of people through their cultures, times and histories, all Divinely inspired by the Holy Spirit!

- The Bible speaks to us through every language and culture that has ever or will exist!

When we are aware of this "tension" between the Bibles language, history and literature, and our perceptions, then we can be careful interpreters. We can be on guard, and be in prayer: So that we are focused on Christ and His Word and not our self.

See appendix A for list of "genres" literature to be aware of.

Be aware of the CONTEXT!!!!!

There are two main areas of "context" we always need to be aware of and ask the text: "what are the "historical" and what are the "literary" settings." That is the content of what is going on in the text. What is going on preceding and after our text, the type[s] of literature, and the various cultural factors? What is the point and train of thought? This in scholarly circles is called "Hermeneutics" the study of interpretation. See Appendix A

1. **The Historical Context:** This is the type of literature "genres" that refer to the time period and culture of the people who wrote it and are writing too. The Locations such as the travels of Paul and Jesus, and the time and the sequence of events. This refers to the "occasion"

and "purpose" of the Authors intention and how and what it means to them and how and what it means to us.

Such as what is the personal background of Isaiah, what was his position {job}, who was he writing to, what were the people like {culture and customs}, what were their expectations are some of the key questions to know what is going on. Careful reading the text and Bible Encyclopedias, Handbooks, and Dictionaries will give you those insights. But make sure you make your own observations first!

2. **The Literary Context:** This is the meaning of the words; the Nouns, Verbs, and Adjectives. Both the meaning of the word[s] itself as well as what they mean in their context of sentence structure and surrounding passages. You can do this quite simply by comparing the word you wish to "dig" by looking at a Concordance and at various translations, such as the word "Denarius" in the Gospels. You may automatically think it is money. And you are right, but what kind of money, what was it used for, what is the amount and its worth are critical questions to understand the meaning of the passage. Be aware that the verse numbers, paragraphs and chapters are not part of the original text!

Discussion:

[This lesson is designed to show the importance of context and how we make mistakes in interpretation when we read the Bible. For this session you need a Concordance, Bible Dictionary, Commentaries, Word Study books, {see Appendix C}, you should be able to find these books in your church library or from your pastor.]

In this lesson we are going to learn the importance of the tools to the Bible and how to use them {try to have the books in hand to show}. When we come to a text that we do not understand or we need to gain new and better insights, we then {only after you pursued the questions to your passage} go to a commentary or "tool!" There are several good sets available.

{From the classic "Matthew Henry," to more modern versions such as, "With the Word" by Wiersbe and "Halley's Bible Handbook." These are single devotional style one volume books, simple to read and understand, and great for general overviews and insights. There are two great study Bibles I recommend, "NIV Study Bible" or the "New Geneva Study Bible," that have a Bible and notes on most of the passages. Then there are multi-volume sets, pick from such solid Biblical publishers, as Tyndale, Inter- Varsity, Zondervan, Moody Press, Eerdmans, Baker, or Thomas Nelson.}

If you do not know which one to choose, ask a pastor you trust. Unfortunately, there is a lot of garbage out there. Beware and be discerning. Always compare Scripture to Scripture, and do not rely just on people's opinions!

- Learning to think "exegetically" will give you a deeper and richer experience in your relationship with Christ. Because you are in a deeper and richer understanding of His Word!

- Your study and reading will become more enjoyable and exciting!

One of the great themes of the Bible is God's love and saving grace to us who do not deserve it!

Remember Too: Make an emotional identification into the text. Place yourself as a participant, being active in it; As if it is your story; As if you are there!

Look up in your Bibles III John.

Read the whole book {it is very short} first in a paraphrase, then the King James, and then the NIV. Ask these questions you have already learned. Remember to overview then take a careful look at a specific verse; verse 2.

- What does this text say?

- What does this text mean?

- What is it saying and what's the meaning in the context?

- Does this text have anything to do with financial prosperity?

- How does it compare to the character of Christ and His teachings?

- Look up in a concordance the key words, "good," "health," "well," and compare them to similar passages. Then look at a Bible that has the references in the margins, and look them up. What did you find? {Sometimes the words we look up have a lot of references. Some, or even most, may not correspond to the text, or there are no references.} Now look up this text in a commentary, what did you find?

- A lot of people teach that this verse means that God will never allow you to get sick, unless you have no faith. Also that God desires you to be wealthy and in good health, and if you are not, there is something wrong with you spiritually. So are they right?

- What rules did they break in their interpretation?

Application:

- How can you know yourself better and your ways of thinking?

- What can you do to guard yourself from making such mistakes?

- It is great to be excited about Scripture! But we must not allow our excitement and expectations to influence bad thinking and bad interpretation.

"Going Deep:"

Read Matthew 5: 3-12 in a paraphrase by candlelight, then remain silent for 3 minutes.

SESSION XII

"Step IV"

Teachers Study: "The responsibility of the Teacher"

Quoting from "Aurelius Augustine of Hippo:"

"The teacher of Holy Scripture must teach what is right and refute what is wrong. In doing this, he must conciliate the hostile, rouse the careless, and tell the ignorant about current events and trends for the future" ... so that his hearers become "friendly, attentive, and ready to learn."

"... the highest priority should be placed on clarity. What advantage is there in speech that does not lead to understanding? Therefore, good teachers avoid all words that do not teach; instead, they must find words that are both pure and intelligible."

"There is an analogy between learning and eating: the very food without which it is impossible to live must be flavored to meet the tastes of the majority."

"To teach is a necessity, to delight is a beauty, to persuade is a triumph."

Lesson Outline:

Remember to begin in prayer!

- Prayer   5 min
- Pick one of the options   5-10 min
- Read lesson and bible passages   10-15min {you can do this and discussions together}
- Discussion groups   15-30 min
- Going deep   5-10 min
- End in prayer and repeat application.   5 min

Total lesson time 45 min- 1 hr

"Options"

Go over the "The Three Essentials of Discipleship" that will endure, "faith, hope, and love—and the greatest of these is love." 1 Cor. 13:13 (NLT)

1. Read I Cor. 13:12 and Col. 1:3-8

2. Then ASK:

Faith is our?
Hope is our?
Love is our?

"Patient endurance is what you need now, so you will continue to do God's will. Then you will receive all that he has promised." {Hebrews 10:36NLT}

"Options"

Read I Cor. 13:12 and Col. 1:3-8 and Heb. 12:1-2a

Committing to a Plan of Growth:

Ask what do we need to do with Faith, Hope, and Love?

1. What do we need to "FIND" _____
"We all have some people around whose lives tell us what faith means, so seek them out!"

2. What do we need to "REMOVE" _____
"We must remove from our lives anything that would get in the way of our Lord, including the sin that holds us back..."

3. What do we need to "FOCUS" _____
"We do this by keeping our eyes on Jesus, as a racehorse has blinders on from keeping it from being distracted, so must we."

Bible, Prayer and Accountability

4. What do we need to "DON'T" _____
"So let us run the race with our focus on the Lord and blinders to everything else and never give up."

{The two options can be combined as the main lesson and do the rest the following week as a break.}

Lesson: "Step IV" QUESTIONS: ASK AND LEARN!!!

Asking questions are the tools to take God's Word and examine it. After this, we learn and grow. Just as a child will learn, so must we for we are God's children. This is the step that goes along side of IIIB and turbo charges it. It causes us to think deeper and gather the additional information we need to be challenged and then to grow.

- When we are challenged to grow, we become better disciples for His kingdom!

Like looking at a great work of art most people who pass it by and make a sly comment, while another person will see the greatness and rave about it. The difference is some people know what to look for. Do you? The same is with the Bible. You will not find much unless you know how to look.

Remember: Effort is essential. You need to put in "Bible Elbow Grease" and the rewards are plentiful. Knowledge is power... God's power for you!

To play baseball, you need a bat. Asking questions is our bat to know God's Word.

"Discussion:"

[Take your passage, {chose a short book like II or III John or Jude or...} and go through it together or in small groups with the questions in this step. Remember whole book first, then chapters then verses.]

THE SIX BIG Q'S WE MUST ALWAYS ASK!

WHO: Who are the people? Who did it? Who can do it? Who is it talking about?

WHAT: What is it saying? What is it talking about? What is happening? What did they do?

WHERE: Where are they going? Where did it happen? Where will it take place?

WHEN: When did it happen? When will it happen? When can it happen?

HOW: How did it happen? How can it happen? How was something done?

WHY: Why did he say that? Why did he do that? Why did they go there?

ASK WHICH ONE OR MORE OF THESE APPLIES.

Note, not all the questions and "STEPS" will apply to every verse, use discernment and common sense, that is good judgment!

MORE TOOLS: GOD'S *WORD IS A PLUMBERS PLUNGER TO THE WORLD'S LEAKING TOILET!*

ASK THESE ADDITIONAL QUESTIONS:

- Are there any commands?

- Are there any contrasts?

- Are there things repeated?

- Is there cause and effect?

- Is there a problem and solution?

- Are there any promises?

- Are there any connections to other parts of the Bible?

- Notice the setting!

You may need to check a Commentary or Bible Encyclopedia on this for some books.

- Compare your verse with other similar verses.

Use your imagination! Let the Bible come alive in you!!!

Check out Appendix C for a list of resources and how to use them.

"Application:"

Ask, can you think of different questions?

- What did you learn?

- How are you going to "make it work" in your life?

"Going Deep:"

A. Spend the remaining time in small group prayer for individual needs and how they can apply what they are learning.

B. Or Meditate {have students read slowly several times quietly with a
   sense of being surrendered to Christ, and not full of the noise of your
   thoughts and plans} on Hebrews 12:1-2a:

*"We have around us many people whose lives tell us what faith
means. So let us run the race that is before us and never give up. We
should remove from our lives anything that would get in the way and the
sin that so easily holds us back. We do this by keeping our eyes on Jesus,
on whom our faith depends from start to finish."* {Heb. 12:1-2a}

SESSION XIII

"Step V"

Teachers Study: "Practical Love"

One of the big signs of an unhealthy church is when the teaching centers on one aspect of truth or one aspect of love, but the two are not taught together as the Bible calls us too. Some churches center on preaching the truth, and do a very good job with it, but they do not have love to balance it out. Other churches model love but do not teach truth. These churches are not modeling the characteristics of God: that God is a God of justice; but also, mercy; the God of law is also a God of grace. We must have a healthy balance of the truth of God's Word and the love of our actions, without this balance the church becomes one-sided and ineffective.

There is a large church in Southern California with a great pastor who I admire very much, I attended this church many times and have had friends that were on staff at this church. But this church has a fatal flaw, it is legalistic. Even though their teaching is correct and "hits the nail on the head" so to speak, it is not practicing the love of Christ, thus many people leave hurt and disillusioned because nobody cared for them there.

The other extreme is another large church in Southern California that has very poor teaching; I would go so far as to label that church as a cult theologically speaking. About 12 years ago I interviewed there to be a youth Pastor, and I was appalled by the questions the senior pastor was giving, and how he was ridiculing me because of my views that Christ was God and Lord. But to be honest this was a very loving and caring church. I felt very comfortable there, and the people were wonderful, open, and accepting; characteristics that all Christians should have, but there is no truth being taught there.

We cannot be so concerned about offending people that we never give the truth, and we should never give the truth without the balance of love. If your church emphasizes love and never speaks of truth, it will collapse. If your church just teaches the truth without the companion of love; then, it will become legalistic and there's one thing a non-Christian cannot stand besides hypocrisy and gossip, its legalism! And you will never reach your community for Christ with a legalistic attitude. Don't get me wrong we are never to confuse legalism as correct theological teaching. Nor are we to compromise the gospel, absolutely not! We are to have a high view of Scripture and communicate God's Word with truth and conviction. What we do not do is boil God's truth down to a list of "dos and don'ts." What we are to do is live out God's love and God's Grace for this communicates the characteristics of Christ more powerfully than a how-to list.

This is God's plan because God loves us. So we must follow through with the principles of Scripture being lived out in our lives. Out of love, out of nurture, out of care, and not out of rules regulations and hatred. Yes we have a God of law as revealed to us throughout Scripture, especially in the Old Testament, and we are under a code, a covenant, a contract, and we need to communicate this effectively within the parameters of love. When we do this, we are teaching the truth. Christianity then becomes a big pill that can be swallowed and not a bad medicine to be avoided.

God's Word tells us, *"instead, speaking the truth in love, we will in all things grow up into Him who is the head, that is Christ. From him the whole body, joined and held together but every supported ligament, grows and builds itself up in love, as each part does its work."* {Ephesians 4:15-16}

How? The solution is simple, follow God's Word. We need to take God's lead and do what He requires with truth, and do it with love. Otherwise, you build yourself a house of cards that will soon fall. The aspects of love and the gifts that God gives us are not for our own private benefit. They are to be shared with one another. God has not called us to be in isolation to each other, but has called us to be in relationship to each other. And the driving force of our relationships is the love that passes all understanding that Christ gives to us, because He is the head; thus, we are to take that love and let it infect those around us. The Christ affected Christian will model Christ and teach the truth in our actions, and our words, and in our deeds, because Christ first loved us.

God's love must be our model for life. It must flow into us by who Christ is, and in return flow out of us to those around us. God's love is the ultimate power for the Christian. We are to be fueled and empowered by love through all situations because Christian love is the turning of our backs to our self-concerns, and then facing forward to our neighbors. If love does not take you beyond your self-interest, then what you have is lust and not love! That love is a principal, that love is an action over against any emotion. That love is a choice, and a lifestyle, and a commitment, and is a trust, love is not a fuzzy feeling in our tummy. Out of true love, God the Father gave us His Son, the Son gave us His life in replacement of our own. The Son sent the Spirit to save us, and we should be literally overwhelmed, and be consumed with extreme joy by what God has done for us.

The Bible tells us in Mark, *"love the Lord your God with all your heart and with all your soul and with all your mind and with all your strength. The second is this: love your neighbor as yourself."* {Mark 12:30-32}

There is no commandment greater than these. Love must unveil our true gratitude and faithfulness to what Christ has done, and in turn let that gratitude flow to our friends, family, and neighbors. The Mark of the Christian life is love, the love that Christ gave us and should be over-flowing in us so that it overflows to those around us. The task of love is how we live our lives with trust and obedience modeling the character Christ. And the manner of that love is how our neighbors view us and respond to us.

{Excerpt from the book, "Pew Sitting" by Richard J. Krejcir}

Lesson Outline:

Remember to begin in prayer!

- Prayer   5 min
- Pick one of the options   5-10 min
- Read lesson and Bible passages   10-15min {you can do this and discussions together}
- Discussion groups   15-30 min
- Going deep   5-10 min
- End in prayer and repeat application.   5 min

Total lesson time 45 min- 1 hr

"Options:"

Have student's list there favorite foods, and have someone write them down on a piece of paper or chalkboard. Then ask them to list the food that they like but are hard to get, such as a fresh fish taco from Mexico, or freshly made "La Cream" chocolate only found in Belgium.

Say: "just as the food we crave may be hard to find or get, God's Word is easy to find and even more delicious. God desires us to desire Him, with passion and conviction, to have a hungry heart for His Word.

Read Psalm 130

"Options:"

[Gather together several things that smell from good to bad {no people} such as spoiled food, after-shave, blue cheese, coffee, dirty socks, road kill, etc.]

Have students either blind folded or have the smelly stuff in paper bags so they cannot see what they smell. Then take turns smelling and guessing the items.

Read II Corinthians 2:14-15

Say: "There are all kinds of smells that are either repulsive or pleasing, these smells bring us the information about them and leaves us with memories to know them.

- The Bible calls us to be a fragrance, so what does your fragrance smell like, is it pleasing or repulsive, or is there a smell at all?

Consider the aroma of the Word. As you read, let it touch you and your memories, to let you "know it" better!

Lesson "Step V:" KNOW IT!!!

Just as the Customs Officer asks you with a deep stern and convicting look when you enter a country, "do you have anything to declare," so must we declare Christ with even more passion and conviction! And we can only do it with knowing it, knowing Him and His Word.

This is the step that helps us "internalize" what we are learning. This is the process of interpretation, which is determining the meaning of the text. Not just what it says, but what we do with it. Thus when we ask what does it mean, we then need to determine how it's going to "fit into" our life.

You can easily know something without it ever effecting you. Such as watching a tragedy on the news, but never giving it a second thought. We must never allow God's Word to be in that category!!!

It is one thing to believe in the existence of cars, another thing to learn how to drive them. Step IV helps us how to know the existence of cars, or "God's decrees." Step V shows us that we need to take ownership of it, and we must do this before we can drive it. Thus the knowing and internalizing comes before the application. We have to be in tune with what and why we do something before we can do it effectively and grow from it.

It is like a circle, knowing it must precede doing, yet doing can open the door to knowing. And then the knowing will increase the doing…

"It is not enough to just know it. It must be rooted in our very hearts, minds and soul!"

We must ask ourselves, "How can the teaching about God's Word relate to my problems, feelings, values, attitudes, situation, ambitions, needs, desires, and relationships."

START LOOKING FOR THE ANSWERS:

"Interpretation" is the process of determining the meaning of the text.

You cannot make an application until you are a "new life" that is we must be the people of God to be able to do the work of God!

Be aware:

You will get into big trouble if you try to read into the text what is not there! A lot of Christians and even some pastors today like to find "secret meanings" from the text. Thus books like the "Bible Code" become popular. But there is no code other than the one made up by its authors by backward engineering a formula into the text. And their formula does not work or have any consistency.

- THERE ARE NO SECRET MEANINGS {except some apoplectic writings, but they are not a "secret" just temporally hidden, they will be plainly revealed in time}!!!!

- You are not to dig out what is not there. You are not to send your "ferret" {a rodent that likes to hunt for things, similar to a mink} mind to bring back what is not there. Can I be any clearer?

WHAT YOU WANT TO DO IS:

Discover and understand what the divine author means.

Example: When Jesus says He is the bread of life, does this mean He is the loaf of bread?

Be Aware of the Context!!!

Like cutting a beautiful flower and studying it as if it were a whole plant and ignoring the stems, roots and leaves. The flower will wither and die without the nourishment from the rest of the plant. So it is when we take a verse out of its context!

Study the verses better and slowly. Are you taking something out of its context? The chapter and verses **are not inspired**. The publisher, to make reading easier, has added them in.

"Discussion:" THINGS TO VIEW, ASK, AND TO APPLY:

Take your passage, {choose a short book like II or III John or Jude or...} and go through it together or in small groups with these steps.

1. Ask WHAT DOES SOMETHING MEAN AND WHY IS IT THERE?

- Discover the historical and cultural background.

- Be sure your information is correct! Use good commentaries, Study Bibles, and Bible dictionaries.

2. Digging Personally:

- How are you encouraged and strengthened?

- Where have you fallen short, and how can you improve?

- What do you now intend to do with the information given to you by the Holy Spirit through God's Word?

Remember: *"All scripture is inspired by God and profitable for teaching..."* We must never substitute doctrine for personal beliefs! (II Timothy 3:16)

"Application:"

- How can you guard yourself from finding things in the Bible that are not there?

- **Read,** *"Now the Bereans were of more noble character than the Thessalonians, for they received the message with great eagerness and examined the Scriptures every day to see if what Paul said was true."* {Acts 17:11}

- Ask how can you do this?

"Going Deep:"

Read {or have someone else read} the following, have students close their eyes:

When you look at a gourmet cooking magazine, you will notice all kinds of adjectives such as "The Best, Favorite, Fine, Superb, Blissful, Great, Fantastic, Incredible, Perfect, Pleasingly," and I could go on and on! These adjectives are describing and expressing the enthusiasm and quality of the food. From the way it is prepared to the way it is presented to the guest. All centering around the experience coming from the work, effort and quality put into it by the chef.

When we are reading God's Word, we are a chef preparing a marvelous and fantastic feast, what we get will be what we put into it, from the quality of the ingredients to the time it takes to cook will determine how transformed you will be!

To receive any true benefit from scripture we have to be in it deeply and earnestly. Plunging ourselves into the depths of the words and details.

To receive our profit from our investment, we must seize the adjectives with enthusiasm and vigor, like partaking in your favorite meal, from its aroma to its taste and consumption!

Taking the aroma of the words and keep at it until the taste and meaning are enveloping and transforming your life!

- Getting into God's Word must affect our every day life. How we think, how we feel. This is where our values come from.

- We are to be active in God's Word even when we are not reading it.

- A life based on analysis, synthesis, valuing, organizing, and comprehending our Lord Jesus Christ.

- To our very "existential core" that is the soul and being of who we are to Christ!

- We must have the confidence that the Bible is truth, and the truth is living within us.

Without such confidence, we can no way transform ourselves, let alone infect others with the Gospel message! This is Knowing It!

- WE must allow God's Word to bend and break our will and desires over to His!

What did God say to you today?

What did God nourish with you today?

Are you appreciating it?

Are you not only receiving the great benefits, but practicing them to others around you?

Are you a changed person as a result of receiving the Word?

- Service is who we are in Christ, and not so much what we do for Christ!

Do not skip your meals in God's Word!

Session XIV

"STEP VI"

Teachers Study:

One of the main problems of why Christians go bad in their motives and behaviors is that they forget who they are. Too many people who go to church have not a clue of what it is about. Perhaps they once did when the excitement of their new birth in Christ was new and they were growing. But now the noise and busyness of life took over the time slot that was originally reserved for God. So our time and excitement of church becomes clouded, preventing us from remembering what it is supposed to be about. So we forget who we are and what we are called to do.

Thus, week by week we hurry ourselves and drag the family to go to church, through the tyranny of the daily grind and sit in our pews, trying to recover from the exhaustion, hoping our struggle is not in vain. Thus we give little effort to what the words mean when we sing a hymn, what the pastor is talking about at the pulpit, or the beauty of the liturgy and the power and conviction of the words. We are just playing a part in a play without allowing the character to become who we are. Without allowing the purpose of what is going on, the meaning of the service, and the application we are called to respond to get in us. So then church becomes just a routine and not the church that Christ created for us to be.

One of my favorite stories of the old west, is the tail of the Alamo. This is one of the best examples of courage I have ever encountered. In Texas on March the sixteenth, 1836 at 6:30am, the last gunshot was heard, and the Alamo had fallen. After a 13-day siege by over 2000 harden Mexican troops, the bodies of 189 fallen heroes who offered their lives as a last stand to ensure the freedom of Texas. Colonel William Travis, the commander of the fort, was possibly the first to fall while defending the north wall. He was only 26. Jim Bowie, who is known for his very cool knife, was the commander. But, he turned over the command to Travis because he was sick and totally exhausted for standing against the Mexican army for several days and he was possibly dying of pneumonia. He was killed in his bed. He was 41. And Davy Crockett, with a cool raccoon hat, the most famous of them all, went to Texas to help them win their freedom, after he had lost his farm and political carrier as a territorial Governor. He was killed in a small fort to the southwest. He was 50. And 186 others lay fallen by the hopeless odds, and the bold determination that they could prevail.

Colonel Travis was hoping for a garrison of reinforcements, but knew they would arrive too late. So he told his men that they could leave because it was clear they would surely die. Or he said they could stay and make a stand and certainly be killed. So he drew a line in the dirt and anybody that wanted to stay could join him across the line. One soldier, who was already wounded and could not fight asked to be carried over the line, then every one except 1 volunteer joined Travis to stay to the bitter end. The one soldier, who did not stay, carried their story, or we would have never known what happened. Over 600 Mexican troops lay dead. The rest were killed or captured by Sam Houston on April 21st. and won the freedom for Texas.

There are times when courage is called for, when we need to go beyond ourselves in an extraordinary fashion, and a leap of faith. Most acts of courage have been associated with military feats, or with acts of persecution. But God calls us, the average Christian, to the same act of courage that the men at the Alamo exhibited. We may not have to give our physical lives, but we are expected to give ourselves fully to the Lordship of Christ. Too many Christians forget we have been enlisted in an army, and are called to defend the fort. We may not be using guns and artillery, but we have the biggest weapon of all, the power of the Holy Sprit, and the model of love and care to be shown to the world. We are to prevail no matter what the odds may be, or the circumstances we may face, because our hope and courage comes directly from our Lord. He arms us with His presence, and empowers us with His Spirit.

There may be times where we are called to take a stand and be persecuted, and even physically die. But most Christians will never see such persecution, but we will see our family, friends, and neighbors in distresses that need to be protected and saved. When we sit in our pews and do nothing, would be like the men of the Alamo deciding to give up and leave. And if that happened, Santa Ana and his Mexican troops would have overrun Texas because the people were fragmented and not sold on the idea of independence. So the battle cry, "remember the Alamo" would never have galvanized the people of Texas to fight for their freedom, and Texas today would probably be part of Mexico! And perhaps the oil and industrial moderation of the early twentieth century would have happened south of the border: Because Mexico would have had most of the resources to be a world power.

Just a thought from history and what could have happened, and how a small group of people or even just one person can make a difference for our Lord. Too many Christians have decided to make their stand in the pews, with their rear ends firmly planted, and complain that the morals of our society have gone array. Our society has gone array because we have gone array. The troops of the opposition have overrun our country and world because we decided to leave the fort, and have forsaken our call. Just take a trip to Europe and see all the empty magnificent churches, and the decadent and lost societies, whose people find no meaning in life, and seek just like Europe in a generation. {Excerpt from the book, "Pew Sitting" by Richard J. Krejcir}

"OPTIONS"

A. "Balloon Strobe Dance"

This is a variation of a popular youth group game, "Balloon Stomp." Where you tie balloons around the ankles and have everyone try to stomp on others balloons while keeping theirs safe. Here is a variation with an insight.

First do this game as you normally do, then get a strobe light and turn off all the lights in the room and do it again. This is incredibly fun and incredibly difficult. Try not to spend too much time with this, 10 minutes max.

Introduce the lesson by saying, "When we try to do something in the proper light, it can be simple and easy. If we try to do the same task in the wrong light, we will not be able to do it well. This is true when we try to apply God's Word into our lives. When we know what we are doing and why we are doing it, we will get more out of it and be better used by our Lord. When we try to do something with bad intentions or a bad attitude, we will mess it up. Our proper light is who we are in Christ that we belong to Him. The improper light is thinking that we are the masters of our own domain. We may be able to do some "civil" application from His Word, but what good will it do, and who does it benefit?"

B. "Why are devotions important?"

If you try getting a good grade in class without studying the subject, without attending class, without taking notes, without doing your homework, without reading the textbook, how well will you do in that class? If you do some of the requirements, say you attend the class but take no notes or read the textbook, how well will you do? Lets say you do everything well, attend all the classes, take careful notes, do your homework, but never bother opening the textbook, how well will you do?

Well this is how most Christians live their Christian walk. Either they ignore all the "work," do a couple of things, or maybe do it all, but never read the Word, how good will they be as a disciple? God may not give us grades and gold stars now, but He does have a plan for us and a reward in the end. There are some key principles to being a committed disciple, such as prayer, devotions, attending a good church, and Bible study. And when we do some, none, or leave out just one, we will become weak and falter in our walk with our Lord.

If you do not attend a good church or do any devotions, and then expect to be blessed by God, you will find disappointment. If you are just doing 2 of the 4 key principles of being a disciple, but you are not communicating with God, you will find yourself running into discouragement. Then, you cannot be a mature Christian unless you have all four of these principles. Without being in God's Word, you will not mature in the faith and grow in His knowledge. You must do all four to be a mature disciple that God will use greatly.

Can He still use you if you only do some? Well of course He can and will. But how much more and what greater impact will you have in others lives, and yourself when you are complete and centered as His disciple. How much more will we be blessed in the Christian walk to further His kingdom.

Lesson: "STEP VI" APPLICATION!!!

This is the step where the rubber of the tires meets the road. All the previous five steps lead up to this. This is the main point of why we study the Bible, to do something with it. Of course we all do something with it, either we ignore it or we are transformed by it.

We can master all the previous steps, even be transformed by the Word; but, if nothing comes from it, it is meaningless and nearly worthless. This is one of the main points of the book of James. Our faith must have a response to it. Yes we may be saved, but what good is it if we do nothing with it.

With the knowledge we have learned, it becomes our responsibility! And then we are to ask, "how then do I live?" What can I do now, today, or this week to implement the instructions given to me with my relationship to Christ, to others, and to myself?

True application comes only from the result of a life transformed. You may do good works without Christ, but they are out of a sense of obligation and guilt, and not out of a response to our sin nature that has been covered by grace creating a willing and loving heart to model the character of our Lord!

- The fruits of the Spirit are the result of a life transformed by Christ.

How we are un-transformed: *"The acts of the sinful nature are obvious: sexual immorality, impurity and debauchery; idolatry and witchcraft; hatred, discord, jealousy, fits of rage, selfish ambition, dissensions, factions and envy; drunkenness, orgies, and the like. I warn you, as I did before, that those who live like this will not inherit the kingdom of God."* {Gal. 5:19-21}

How we are transformed: *"But the fruit of the Spirit is love, joy, peace, patience, kindness, goodness, faithfulness, gentleness and self-control.*

Against such things there is no law. Those who belong to Christ Jesus have crucified the sinful nature with its passions and desires. Since we live by the Spirit, let us keep in step with the Spirit. Let us not become conceited, provoking and envying each other." {Gal 5:22-26}

- God uses His Word to transform us, it is what we do, and what He does. He sends us His Spirit, we respond.

REMEMBER: Application comes out of a Changed life and leads to a life transformed! Rom 12:1-3

SOMETHING TO CONSIDER:

- Satan would like nothing better than for you not to do the above!!! Do not procrastinate. Press on!!! Do not assume that because you understand something that you have applied it!!! Do not get frustrated. You cannot expect instant results.

- Studying the Word without putting any application to it is like buying a nice new car, taking it home and keeping it in your garage. Then all you do is sit in it and pretend you are driving, listening to the radio, but never actually turning it on and going anywhere with it.

- When we read God's Word and do nothing with it, we become the biggest fools in the universe!

- This area of putting feet to God's Word is the most neglected aspect of our Christian life! But it is at this part where our lives change and God uses us to change others.

"Discussion:" THINGS TO VIEW, ASK, AND APPLY:

Take your passage, {choose a short book like II or III John or Jude or...} and go through it together or in small groups with these steps.

1. Jesus urged us to build our lives on His Word. (See Matthew 7:24-27)

- What must I do to make God's Word real in me?

- When will what I learned end up in my day planner?

- What is my response?

- The Word of God is to lead us to model the character of Christ, to be formed in the image of God.

Mediate over the passage you are studying, that is reflect on it, ponder it, and think of it so that you are seriously going over the passage over and over in your mind. Then the memorization will become easier since the verse[s] have rooted in you!

Then the life transformed will take effect much easier and completely!

ASK YOURSELF THESE FIVE QUESTIONS:

1. What illustration or analogy can I develop to remember the truth it contains?

2. How does the truth apply to my life?

3. What is my personal prayer regarding these truths? Write it out and present it to the Lord.

4. What changes/improvements could I make in light of the truth? List several.

5. How should I carry out these changes?

    If no application comes to your mind, pray, and pray again. Let God show you His way, not our way.

"Application:" Pick one

A. "The **Big Tip**" {Get several tape recorders and tapes.} Have student practice **Reading Their Bible passages and verses into a Tape Player.** This is so they can learn **to memorize Scripture!**

    You can do this with NOTES, TEXT, READINGS, etc. Then, play it back while driving, or at the mall, or anywhere, with a "Walk-Man." You can do this with any of your notes, study material, information you have to memorize, even terms and words for science or a foreign language, or math formulas. This is one of the best ways to study!!!!!!!!!!!!! THIS WORKS!!!!!!!!!!!

B. How can you:

- **Pray** to ask God how to implement His truth to you.

- **Tell Others.** Remember Matthew 28. The best way to remember what you learn is to teach others.

- **Accountability.** Let someone else you know and trust hold you to your promises especially as it relates to the study of God's Word.

Beware!! The more knowledge we have, the more accountability and responsibility we have to God. This is why Moses was not allowed into the Promised Land, when he seemingly disobeyed God by hitting a rock with his staff. It may not seem much of an offense to us, but before God, Moses knew better then anyone else. Fortunately for us today, we have grace!

"Going Deep:"

Have a student read the following passages {it is always better focused to go deep by turning out the lights and light a candle}:

"*But it has now been revealed through the appearing of our Savior, Christ Jesus, who has destroyed death and has brought life and immortality to light through the gospel. And of this gospel I was appointed a herald and an apostle and a teacher. That is why I am suffering as I am. Yet I am not ashamed, because I know whom I have believed, and am convinced that he is able to guard what I have entrusted to him for that day. What you heard from me, keep as the pattern of sound teaching, with faith and love in Christ Jesus. Guard the good deposit that was entrusted to you— guard it with the help of the Holy Spirit who lives in us.*" {II Tim. 1:10-14}

- You can stand in an ice-cream shop all day long and stare at all of the flavors. But no enjoyment or satisfaction will come until you bite into a scoop for yourself!

- Remember the Word of God's purpose is to transform us into the image of God, to model His character!

- Discipleship is following Christ and not just beliefs, ideas, or causes. Too many people are devoted to a doctrine or a cause in the name of

Christ, but not Christ Himself! That is how we got the Inquisition and Crusades.

"For this reason I remind you to fan into flame the gift of God, which is in you through the laying on of my hands. For God did not give us a spirit of timidity, but a spirit of power, of love and of self-discipline. So do not be ashamed to testify about our Lord, or ashamed of me his prisoner. But join with me in suffering for the gospel, by the power of God, who has saved us and called us to a holy life—not because of anything we have done but because of his own purpose and grace. This grace was given us in Christ Jesus before the beginning of time." {I Tim. 1:6-9}

SESSION XV

"STEP VII"

Teachers Study: "The Response of us, the Church"{Judges 6:1-6}

The question is how do we respond to the call of the church, and the walk of our faith? The people of Israel when occupied after Joshua's death hid in caves, because they forgot they were the people of God, and forgot the power of their God. Since they forgot God, they disobeyed their covenant and did evil. So an invading army took over their land, with one of the most graphic descriptions in the Bible. They neglected their responsibility and then suffered the consequence. Not because of a vengeful God, but because they did not follow God's instructions on how to build their country. So they were unable to defend it, and most important to rely and trust on their God, and not themselves and false idols.

So God sends them a prophet, and tells the people of Israel not to fear, but to trust in the Lord. He reminds them where they came from and how their God brought them out of Egypt, and out of slavery into a land filled with homes, farm lands, orchards, vineyards, and even cities ready for them to move in to. Their only call was to respond out of gratitude, trust, and honor, and obey the Lord their God. The people needed to wake up and see their situation and the history that brought them there. That the fear they have for the Midians is misplaced, and they need to fear the Lord. A fear of respect and judgment, if they do not yield to the obedience of the Lord.

We need to be careful that we do not forget who we are, and what God calls us to do. We should take heed from this passage and to the situation in the church. That hiding in cave or sitting in pews in fear of what ever it may be is not the obedience that Christ paid for. Until an angel came to him, Gideon was hiding his wheat in a winepress so the invading armies could not find it. This Angel gave him his orders to be a warrior, but Gideon gave all kinds of objections and excuses why he could not under take the call. We too give God all kinds of excuses why we cannot do it, and as God was patient with Gideon, He is also patient with us. But nevertheless we have the call and the ability to respond; this is what we must do.

God does not promise us peace, wealth and prosperity, this is not found in scripture, only in the minds of false teachers. What God does promise us is Himself. God's promise is His presence and His power; our peace and prosperity will come in the life after. We have the ability to succeed and overcome if only we obey and respond to Him. When we really believe that God is with us, then the church will become reverent, and the reason to go will be powerful and compelling. We need to get over our fears of what may happen, and respond to build a church, so people do want to come to it. God does not call us to be the church of obnoxiousness, but the church militant. That is we are called to care and love with passion and fervor, not a church of cowards who does nothing but cause strife.

We cannot compromise our values and teaching because we are afraid to offend. And we cannot practice the truth without love and care. We are not to be the offenders, only the gospel may offend. Our job is to show the courage of the Alamo, and the battle cry of Gideon. Just as Gideon woke up to his situation and call, so must we. For us to succeed, we must respond to the glory of our Lord, put off the fear, and put on the courage to serve. Remember Jesus Himself tells us to fear not numerous times in scripture, and it is always an imperative, that is a command! {Excerpt from the book, "Pew Sitting" by Richard J. Krejcir}

"Options:"

Go over these 4 "calls" that show of the necessity of Evangelism Missions, and outreach:

1. People are "sick" and infected with sin. This means we are all are separated from God and this leads to death {Rom. 3:23}.

2. God wants everyone to be saved, but not every one will be {John 3:16}.

3. God works through us, the ordinary Christian, to help others {Matt. 28:18-20}.

4. Each person must make a decision of faith, which is first empowered by the Spirit {Gal. 4:6; Rom. 8:14-27}.

"Options:"

Break out those maps or, better yet, get some to exotic locations, perhaps from AAA, a "Rand McNally" store, or the Internet.

- Ask the students to plan a dream trip to any location.

- Where would it be?

- Why did you choose that place?

- What do you think you need for it?

Lesson "STEP VII:" CHARTING YOUR PATH "Learning to use the Chart"

This is the step where you keep track of what you learn. Pastors get better at preaching and teaching not just by practice and study, but also by going over what they taught in the past. Playing their tapes, re-reading, and reviewing their studies. They can see where they have been to go further ahead. It also acts as an archive of learning, a database of what we have learned that we can draw from.

By writing it down in an organized fashion, God's Word will become more clear and crisp. We are able to record what God says to us, this way we will be able to take more ownership and then greater transformation. We will be able to look back and see and remember what we have discovered. It will make us better disciples, children of God, and teachers of the Word. It will show you how to apply the principles to your life and others! And of course be able to remember more!

We then can look back and see God at work in our lives and will be a great encouragement in times of struggle, and in times of joy. You can review a passage you did in the past and see how you have learned and grown, and quickly brush up on passages that you are being taught from others.

A BOOK CHART WILL HELP YOU GREATLY

- This is where you write down what you learn from the previous steps.

- It will allow you to see a whole book at a glance.

- It will allow you to reach and remember what you learn much, much faster and better.

- It will reveal the theme of a chapter or paragraph just at a glance.

THIS CHART IS IN FOUR (4) SECTIONS

1ST: "Chapter and paragraph titles."
2nd: "Observation:" "What does it say?"
3rd: "Observation:" "What does it mean?" Ask what are the implications.
4th: "Application:" "How does it apply to my life?" This is where we use Steps V & VI.

"Discussion:" THINGS TO VIEW, ASK, AND APPLY:

Choose a short book like Philemon or Jude and go through it together or in small groups, and try to chart the whole book. It may be rough and rushed, but they may learn how to get started on it!

1ST: "Chapter and paragraph titles." This is were you can summarize chapters and whole books in your own words or paraphrase a verse[s]. You can create an outline of the passage by making your own tittles for paragraphs and insights. STEPS I and II come into play here!

- Develop your own chapter and paragraph titles.

- Be creative. Try harder.

- Be sure it describes the passage and relates to it!

- Do not be too general.

- Keep them short so they are easy to remember.

Use your individual unique way of expressing yourself.

2nd: "Observation:" "What does it say?" This is where you use STEP III, and write your observations.

- Bible Statements.

- Who, What, Where, When, How, and Why.

3rd: "Observation:" "What does it mean?" This is where you use STEPS IIIB & IV.

- Ask what are the implications.

- Ask your questions here!

4th: "Application:" "How does it apply to my life?" This is where we use Steps V & VI.

- How does it apply to my life?

- How can I implement God's Word into my life?

- What will I do with this information?

- **When will I do it?**

"OTHER INFORMATION" This is where you can write down your prayers and doodles.

Remember to Pray!!!

REMEMBER: WHEN YOU READ THE BIBLE:

- Pray, pray, pray! Be continuously in prayer as you read His Word.

- Ask questions.

- Use all the previous six-(6) steps when applicable.

- Then write it down. Do not want to use this book chart, then keep a diary or notebook.

Do not hesitate to record other useful information, especially your prayers!!

REMEMBER:

- Study the chapters and paragraphs first!!!

- Then write your outline. You can do this by assigning names for the paragraphs. Use steps I through VI.

"Application:"

- What did you find your application to be?

- How can you do it?

"Going Deep:"

Break into groups of two and share with each other what you have learned in this series, and what you hope to gain in the future.

Or practice "solitude."

APPENDIX A

"What are the types of Literature "genres" in the Bible"?

The Bible is not one "book," it is a "library" of sixty-six books that were written over a period of more than a 1,500 years by many different authors. These authors were "inspired" in their thinking and writing by the Holy Spirit. Thus the Bible is the inspired Word of God without error. It also has the human "touch" from its authors. Paul is different than David, who is different than James or Moses. So their "style and personality comes out to us. This creates the marvelous depth and wonder of Scripture and of how God chooses to use us when He does not need to.

The Bible is Literature, as is any book filled with language. It has: Law, History, Wisdom, Poetry, Gospel, Epistles, Prophecy, and Apocalyptic Literature.

Law is "God's law," they are the expressions of His sovereign will and character. The writings of Moses contain a lot of Law. God provided the Jews with many laws {619 or so}. These laws defined the proper relationship with God to each others and the world {the alien}: As well as worshipping God, governing the people, priestly duties, what to eat and not eat, how to build the temple, proper behavior, manners, and social interaction, etc. The Ten Commandments are often known as "The Law," so are Exodus, Leviticus, Numbers, and Deuteronomy. In the NT, the Sermon on the Mount is considered law and the fulfillment of the law. Paul's "calls" or precepts to the church are also law in their literature form.

Most Christians have a distorted view of the law and think it does not apply to us. Jesus repeated and affirmed the Ten Commandments and the Law of Moses. The law points to our depravity and need for a Savior. Without the law, there would be no relationship to God or need for Christ to save us. Christ fulfills the law and thus we are not bound to its curse, but we must acknowledge its role in our lives as the pointer to the Cross, and the mirror to our soul.

History. Almost every OT book contains history. Some books of the Bible are grouped together and commonly referred to as the "History" {Joshua, Kings & Chronicles}. These books tell us the history of the Jewish people from the time of the Judges through the Persian Empire. In the NT, Acts contains some of the history of the early church, and the Gospels also have History as Jesus' life is told as History. Even the Epistles have history as they chronicle events.

Wisdom Literature is focus on questions about the meaning of life {Job, Ecclesiastes}, practical living, and common sense {Proverbs and some Psalms }. This literature contrasts our faulty human wisdom to God's reasoning perfection. Thus when we live to our own will and not His, we will experience grief and frustration, not because God is vengeful and angry but because we led ourselves that way out of our pride and arrogance. This literature warns us of our evil nature and desires.

Poetry is found mostly in the Old Testament and is similar to modern poetry. Since it is a different language, "Hebrew," the Bible's poetry can be very different, because it does not translate into English very well. Poetry that we are used to is usually based on "rhythm" or various types of sound mixings such as our music. Hebrew poetry is based on "rhythm" of stanzas and phrases re-told differently, conveying the same ideas and meaning. Some Bible books are all poetry {Psalms, Song of Songs, and Lamentations}, and some Books only have a few verses such as in Luke.

Gospel means the "good news" that we received through salvation by the work and life of God's Son, Jesus Christ. When the Gospels were first written in the first century, it was a brand new form of literature. The four Gospels {Mark, Matthew, Luke, and John} contain a bit of all the literary types with the primary purpose to express faith in Christ and what He has done on our behalf. Each of the gospels present the teachings, ministry, death, and resurrection of Jesus in a distinctive way, but not contradictory for a specific audience. Matthew was written to Jews, Luke to the Greeks, both with different ways of reasoning and thinking. Think of the Gospels like the facets of a diamond, giving more depth and meaning.

Epistles refer to the 21 letters in the NT. These are the personal letters by the apostles to their churches. These letters are different and similar to the letters of their time. Most challenge the congregation to wake up out of their selfish ways and to concentrate on Christ with specific ways and clarifications. They begin with the name of the writer and the recipient, a greeting, a reason for the letter, the central message or body of the letter, and then usually a closing, just like most letters today.

The epistles deal with concerns and false teaching that needed imme-diate correction. Some epistles were written in response to questions from the church, or for clarification to another letter, such as II Corinthians. The teachings of the epistles apply both to the church that they were written to, and to Christians today. However, we need to understand the cultural and historical situation to better understand what is going on, so we do not misunderstand what is being said.

Prophecy is the type of literature that is often associated with predicting the future; however, it is also God's words of "get with it" or else. Thus Prophecy also exposes sin and calls for repentance and obedience. It shows how God's law can be applied to specific problems and situations, such as the repeated warnings to the Jews before their captivity. This is found in the OT books of Isaiah through Malachi, the section of the Bible labeled "Prophecy" by both Jews and Christians. There are over 2000 predictions that have already come to pass, hundreds of years after the author's death!

In the NT, prophecy is mainly found in the book of Revelation. Prophecy has both an immediate call to a given situation, such as the "seven churches of Revelation," and a predated future to come to pass. That is it has two folds, a past and a future; both applying to the present. Some predictions are already fulfilled, such as with the birth, life, death, and resurrection of Jesus Christ, and some is yet to come to pass such as sections of Daniel and Revelations and the return of Christ.

Apocalyptic Writing is a more specific form of prophecy. Apocalyptic writing is a type of literature that warns us of future events which, full meaning, is hidden to us for the time being. Apocalyptic writing is almost a "secret" giving us glimpses through the use of symbols and imagery of what is to come. We may not know the meanings now, but time will flush it out. Apocalyptic writing is found in Isaiah, Daniel, Ezekiel, Zechariah, and Revelation.

Warning, a lot of Christian writers love to embellish on this subject and give their own version of what will happen. But the scores of books that have been written in the last hundred years have not paned out in their theories. It is "their" theory, not based on fact or careful study of scripture. The Bible clearly tells us we do not have access to that information, no one will know the time...

For more in-depth and insightful look into the "genres" and knowing the Bible see the resources: "How to read the Bible for all its Worth" by Fee, Zondervan; and "Knowing Scripture" by R.C. Sproul, Inter Varsity. And for the serious student or seminarian, "Exegetical Fallacies" by D.A. Carson, Baker; and "Biblical Exegesis" by Hayes, John Knox Press.

Appendix B

"About all those different versions, and translations"

Remember the Bible was written in Hebrew for most of the Old Testament, and Greek for the New Testament. So there are always many ways to translate a different language.

The main Bible Translations:

KJV: The Kings James is over 400 years old and the language means and reads different than what we are used to, so unless you are an English "Lit" major working on your Ph.D., then read it for its beauty and not for study. You can observe this yourself by watching old TV shows from the 50's and listen how they used language and compare it to now. Big difference, hence why kids today laugh at those shows differently than the original intention was. Now a translation from the 50's would be hard to understand, so what of 400 years past?

NKJV: The New King James Version {1982}, This is an excellent translation and very readable.

NASB: New American Standard Bible {1960}, an excellent translation for serious study word for word translation, which translates each word from the original language into the best corresponding English equivalent. However it is wooden and hard to read. It is a favorite among conservative evangelicals.

NIV: New International Version {1973}, a very readable Bible, it is a cross between a "word for word" translation and a "Dynamic translation" which brings additional words into the text to make the point of the original language. This is often necessary because when you translate any language, you cannot always do it word for word and convey the original thought from the speaker or author. This version has some of the finest American scholarships. Make this Bible your best friend!

RSV: Revised Standard Version {1952}, the standard pew Bible until the NIV. Good translation but word usage will be hard to understand and is dated {i.e. 50's TV show}. Words lose and gain different meanings from generation to generation. This translation is two generations removed from us today.

NRSV: New Revised Standard Version {1991}, is very poor and very excellent scholarship, so unless you can determine the difference stay away. This version reads into the text theological agendas that are not there, stay far away from it!

NAB: New American Bible {1970} this is the best Catholic Bible, excellent scholarship.

NLT: New living Translation {1999} is an excellent cross between a translation and a paraphrase. Make this Bible your second best friend!

JB: Jerusalem Bible {1966} is an English translation of a French translation {Bible de Jerusalem}. It is not translated from the original languages! However it is very poetic and beautiful with its use of language, but not so good of a translation. It is great for extra insights.

NEB: The New English Bible {1961} great English scholarship from the folks who brought us fish and chips, thus is filled with "British Idioms," so you may not understand it well, unless you watch a lot of British TV. It is great insightful reading, especially the Psalms, but use only next to a literal translation NASB, NIV or NKJV.

LB: The Living Bible {Translated in 60's Pub in 1971} Great easy reading for reading the Bible like a novel, but far from the literal meaning. Use the updated version; NLT.

GNB. The Good News Bible {1966} is a paraphrase with very good scholarship, brings the Bible easy to read, excellent to get the big picture and along side of a good translation.

Some other good insightful paraphrases are J.B. Philips {1947}, Moffit {1900's}, The Amplified Bible {1958}, The Message {1993}, Contemporary English Version"{1995} this is great for youth and children or teaching them, or the "New Century Version" {1987}.
And there are hundreds more!

Here is a chart to show approximately how literal they are:

Literal {word for word} / A Cross Some what literal / Dynamic {extra emphases} / Paraphrase

NASB	NKJV		NEB	NLT		LB
RSV	NIV	NRSV	JB		CEV	Philips
KJV		NAB {catholic}			GNB	Amplified

APPENDIX C

"The Tools and resources you need to Know!"

These are the book resources to help you to understand the text, meanings, and historical circumstances, so you can get more out of your studies. These are also available in computer software form, which makes the job fast and easy!

Concordance: This is the "Yahoo" and "Hot Boot" of the Bible, so you can take a key word and find out the passages that you want and others that expand on it. This resource is a complete alphabetical listing of all the words in the Bible. It relates the principle themes, doctrines, and ideas. It works just like an Internet search without the clicking. Let's say you remember a verse that said something about "wings of eagles," but you did not know how to find it. Just look up the key words, "eagle" and then "wings" and visit the sites, i.e. passages until you get to the one you want. Sometimes it can be hundreds like prayer, or just a few like 8 for "eagle" or 7 for "wings," it is easy!

A concordance can be very helpful to clarify word meanings, by looking them up in their various contexts; in doubt look it up!

Commentaries: They are designed to expand on the thoughts of the passage through original language study, historical information, settings, and in-depth study by learned scholars with various viewpoints. There are many good and bad commentaries. See your pastor who is knowledgeable and teaches correctly, he may recommend some. I recommend for students, the "NIV Bible Commentary" by Zondervan and "The IVP Bible Background Commentary" by IVP press. The Bible Exposition Commentary" by Wiersbe is very basic and insightful. Then there are multi-volume sets. Pick from such solid Biblical publishers, as Tyndale, Inter- Varsity, Zondervan, Moody Press, Eerdmans, Baker, or Thomas Nelson.

Ask a pastor you trust because, unfortunately, there is a lot of garbage out there. Beware and be discerning, always compare Scripture to Scripture, and do not rely just on people's opinions!

Study Bibles: These are Bibles with some basic notes to help you dig deeper into the text. I recommend the "New Geneva Study Bible" and the "NIV Study Bible."

Do not solely rely on commentaries and study Bibles. Nothing beats study for yourself because you will get addicted to rely on them and, thus, get lazy on your personal studies! Use the commentaries just to see what you may have missed, and what you do not understand!

Bible Dictionary and Bible Encyclopedia: These work just like a standard dictionary or encyclopedia, with the exception of words and topics found in scripture. This can be a great tool to find out more information, subjects, and terms to understand what is being said or what is going on. Baker and Zondervan have several good ones to choose from.

Maps: Most Bibles have maps in them and they are designed so you know where stuff is going on, it gives you a "where" perspective, especially in the book of Acts where there is a lot of traveling.

Books about the Bible: These books help the student to understand what the Bible is about and give general overviews. Such as the classic "What the Bible is All About" by Henrieta Mears founder of "Gospel Light" one of the largest and best producers of Sunday School Curriculums. Also these two works are very helpful: "With the Word" by Warren Wiersbe, provides a devotional overview and "Haley's Bible Handbook" provides overviews and historical facts.

Theological Dictionaries: These books go in-depth with more than just a general understanding of major theological points, such as "Colin-Brown" by Regency and "Evangelical Dictionary of Theology" by Baker.

Appendix D

"Bible Reading CHART!"

Read through the BIBLE in one year!!!

Read the Bible in a Year is a plan to guide your daily Bible reading. Its design allows you to pace yourself and to begin reading at any point of the year (not just January 1).

To help you stay on schedule, consider enhancing your Bible reading by Listening to the Bible being read on cassette as you daily drive in your car, exercise, or work around the house. You can purchase this, borrow it from a library, or read it yourself into a tape recorder!

THE SCHEDULE:

Day 1—Genesis 1-4

Day 2—Genesis 5-8

Day 3—Genesis 9-12

Day 4—Genesis 13-17

Day 5—Genesis 18-20

Day 6—Genesis 21-23

Day 7—Genesis 24-25

Day 8—Genesis 26-28

Day 9—Genesis 29-31

Day 10—Genesis 32-35

Day 11—Genesis 36-38

Day 12—Genesis 39-41

Day 13—Genesis 42-43

Day 14—Genesis 44-46

Day 15—Genesis 47-50

Day 16—Exodus 1-4

Day 17—Exodus 5-7

Day 18—Exodus 8-10

Day 19—Exodus 11-13

Day 20—Exodus 14-16

Day 21—Exodus 17-20

Day 22—Exodus 21-23

Day 23—Exodus 24-27

Day 24—Exodus 28-30

Day 25—Exodus 31-34

Day 26—Exodus 35-37

Day 27—Exodus 38-40

Day 28—Matthew 1-4

Day 29—Matthew 5-6

Day 30—Matthew 7-9

Day 31—Matthew 10-11

Day 32—Matthew 12-13

Day 33—Matthew 14-17

Day 34—Matthew 18-20

Day 35—Matthew 21-22

Day 36—Matthew 23-24

Day 37—Matthew 25-26

Day 38—Matthew 27-28

Day 39—Leviticus 1-4

Day 40—Leviticus 5-7

Day 41—Leviticus 8-10

Day 42—Leviticus 11-13

Day 43—Leviticus 14-15

Day 44—Leviticus 16-18

Day 45—Leviticus 19-21

Day 46—Leviticus 22-23

Day 47—Leviticus 24-25

Day 48—Leviticus 26-27

Day 49—Mark 1-3

Day 50—Mark 4-5

Day 51—Mark 6-7

Day 52—Mark 8-9

Day 53—Mark 10-11

Day 54—Mark 12-13

Day 55—Mark 14

Day 56—Mark 15-16

Day 57—Numbers 1-2

Day 58—Numbers 3-4

Day 59—Numbers 5-6

Day 60—Numbers 7

Day 61—Numbers 8-10

Day 62—Numbers 11-13

Day 63—Numbers 14-15

Day 64—Numbers 16-18

Day 65—Numbers 19-21

Day 66—Numbers 22-24

Day 67—Numbers 25-26

Day 68—Numbers 27-29

Day 69—Numbers 30-32

Day 70—Numbers 33-36

Day 71—Luke 1-2

Day 72—Luke 3-4

Day 73—Luke 5-6

Day 74—Luke 7-8

Day 107—Joshua 11-13

Day 108—Joshua 14-17

Day 109—Joshua 18-20

Day 110—Joshua 21-22

Day 111—Joshua 23-24

Day 112—Acts 1-3

Day 113—Acts 4-5

Day 114—Acts 6-7

Day 115—Acts 8-9

Day 116—Acts 10-11

Day 117—Acts 12-13

Day 118—Acts 14-15

Day 119—Acts 16-17

Day 120—Acts 18-19

Day 121—Acts 20-21

Day 122—Acts 22-23

Day 123—Acts 24-26

Day 124—Acts 27-28

Day 125—Judges 1-3

Day 126—Judges 4-5

Day 127—Judges 6-8

Day 128—Judges 9-10

Day 129—Judges 11-13

Day 130—Judges 14-16

Day 131—Judges 17-19

Day 132—Judges 20-21

Day 133—Ruth 1-4

Day 134—Romans 1-3

Day 135—Romans 4-7

Day 136—Romans 8-10

Day 137—Romans 11-14

Day 138—Romans 15-16

Day 171—2 Kings 4-5

Day 172—2 Kings 6-8

Day 173—2 Kings 9-10

Day 174—2 Kings 11-13

Day 175—2 Kings 14-16

Day 176—2 Kings 17-18

Day 177—2 Kings 19-21

Day 178—2 Kings 22-23

Day 179—2 Kings 24-25

Day 180—2 Corinthians 1-4

Day 181—2 Corinthians 5-9

Day 182—2 Corinthians 10-13

Day 183—1 Chronicles 1-2

Day 184—1 Chronicles 3-4

Day 185—1 Chronicles 5-6

Day 186—1 Chronicles 7-9

Day 187—1 Chronicles 10-12

Day 188—1 Chronicles 13-16

Day 189—1 Chronicles 17-19

Day 190—1 Chronicles 20-23

Day 191—1 Chronicles 24-26

Day 192—1 Chronicles 27-29

Day 193—2 Chronicles 1-4

Day 194—2 Chronicles 5-7

Day 195—2 Chronicles 8-11

Day 196—2 Chronicles 12-16

Day 197—2 Chronicles 17-20

Day 198—2 Chronicles 21-24

Day 199—2 Chronicles25-28

Day 200—2 Chronicles 29-31

Day 201—2 Chronicles 32-34

Day 202—2 Chronicles 35-36

Day 235—Psalms 34-37

Day 236—Proverbs 1-3

Day 237—Psalms 38-42

Day 238—Proverbs 4-7

Day 239—1 Timothy 1-6

Day 240—Psalms 43-49

Day 241—Psalms 50-55

Day 242—Proverbs 8-11

Day 243—2 Timothy 1-4

Day 244—Psalms 56-61

Day 245—Psalms 62-68

Day 246—Proverbs 12-14

Day 247—Psalms 69-72

Day 248—Titus and Philemon

Day 249—Psalms 73-77

Day 250—Psalms 78-80

Day 251—Proverbs 15-17

Day 252—Psalms 81-88

Day 253—Hebrews 1-4

Day 254—Hebrews 5-8

Day 255—Hebrews 9-10

Day 256—Hebrews 11-13

Day 257—Psalms 89-94

Day 258—Psalms 95-103

Day 259—Proverbs 18-20

Day 260—James 1-5

Day 261—Psalms 104-106

Day 262—Psalms 107-111

Day 263—Proverbs 21-23

Day 264—1 Peter 1-5

Day 265—Psalms 112-118

Day 266—Proverbs 24-26

Photo Copy these pages and keep it tucked in your Bible as you plan for your devotional reading!

From: "Into Thy Word"
C 2000 R.J. Krejcir

APPENDIX E

"The cheat sheet"

{Go ahead and photocopy this section and tuck it in your Bible!}

♦ *THE MAIN GOAL OF BIBLE STUDY: DON'T JUST INTERPRET IT, BUT APPLY IT TO YOUR LIFE!!!*

STEP I: *"KNOWING THE KNOWABLE:"* BRINGING OUR MIND TO BE RIGHT WITH GOD!

ATTITUDE is crucial!!! {Gal. 2:20}

♦ REMEMBER TO ALWAYS: BEGIN and END YOUR STUDY IN PRAYER and in the meantime be in prayer.
♦ DIRECT YOUR WILL AND SEIZE THE OPPORTUNITY!!! BE CONSISTENT!!!.
♦ BE OPEN TO THE HOLY SPIRIT

STEP II: "HOW:" THE METHOD OF GETTING INTO GOD'S WORD

LOOK AT THE WHOLE BOOK at least three times in an easy to read translation. Then read each chapter you are studying in a good translation at least three times. Then read the verses, verse by verse in order.

STEP III: "OBSERVE IT:" ASK WHAT DOES IT SAY?! Before you ask what does it mean and how to apply it to your life!

♦ Give the Book the "Looks:" Purpose; Repeated Phrases; The Point; Who is involved; The time & sequence of events, "once, then, now, will be, etc." Look for persons, places, ideas; Logical Connectives, i.e. Therefore, But, Since, So, Thus, Because, For, That, etc. What is actually being said?
♦ Verbs are crucial! Check out **NOUNS** in "Bible Dictionaries."
♦ Consider repeated words & phrases.
♦ Compare passage/verse to similar verses i.e. "Scripture interprets scripture." Use a "Concordance."
♦ Notice what is being taught
♦ Notice the promises
♦ Notice carefully the underlining principle[s] & implications
♦ What about the life, work, teaching, presence of Jesus Christ?
♦ Look out for types of "literary style;" history, philosophy, drama, poetry, wisdom and law.
♦ Look at different translations

STEP III (B): "OBSERVE IT:" ASK WHAT DOES IT MEAN?

Let God have His way with you! Ask our Lord to open you before Him, to allow yourself to go beyond your culture, education and experience! Then the meaning will come alive!

♦ We must know our weaknesses and limitations because of sin!
♦ We must be aware of our nature and the nature of Scripture and the Divine Authors intent.

- Be focused on Christ not ourselves.
- Be aware of the CONTEXT!!!!! The "historical" and "literary" settings?" What is going on?
- What is the point and train of thought?
- ANALYZE by gathering facts and all the information available to you.
- Paraphrase the passage yourself.
- What is supported?
- What are the conclusions?

Make an emotional identification into the text.

THINGS TO ASK AND TO APPLY:
- Ask what is actually being said?
- Try reading aloud!
- Consider nothing insignificant!
- Have a mentor to ask questions.
- Look for stuff to carry out in your life.
- Write down your questions
- What are the implications & promises to be applied to transformed us?
- What about the life, work, teaching, and presence of Jesus Christ?
- How can I model His Character?
- What is our duty?
- What is God's character?
- Make a commitment to the meaning.
- Try to write the verse or entire passage in your own words!
- Accept what It says: This is God's Word!

STEP IV: "QUESTIONS:" ASK AND LEARN!!!

THE SIX BIG Q'S WE MUST ALWAYS ASK!

- **WHO:** are the people? Who did it? Who can do it? Who is it talking about?

- ♦ WHAT: is it saying? What is happening? What is it talking about? What did they do?
- ♦ WHERE: are they going? Where did it happen? Where will it take place?
- ♦ WHEN: did it happen? When will it happen? When can it happen?
- ♦ HOW: did it happen? How can it happen? How was something done?
- ♦ WHY: did he say that? Why did he do that? Why did they go there?

ASK THESE ADDITIONAL QUESTIONS:
- ♦ Are there any commands?
- ♦ Are there any contrasts?
- ♦ Are there things repeated?
- ♦ Is there cause and effect?
- ♦ Is there a problem and solution?
- ♦ Are there any promises?
- ♦ Are there any connections to other parts of the Bible?
- ♦ Notice the setting!

STEP V: "KNOW IT"!!!

START LOOKING FOR THE ANSWERS

- ♦ WHAT DOES SOMETHING MEAN AND WHY IS IT THERE?
- ♦ Be sure your information is correct!!!
- ♦ Use good commentaries, Study Bibles, and Bible dictionaries.

Digging Personally:
- ♦ How are you encouraged & strengthened?
- ♦ Where have you fallen short, and how can you improve?
- ♦ What do you now intend to do with the information given to you?
- ♦ We must have the confidence that the Bible is truth! This is knowing It!
- ♦ We must allow God's Word to break our will and desires over to His!
- ♦ What did God say to you today?
- ♦ Is there a sin in your life that needs to be confessed and repented?

♦ Are you appreciating it?
♦ Are you receiving and practicing the great benefits to others around you?
♦ Are you a changed person as a result of receiving the Word?

STEP VI: "APPLICATION!!!" {Gal 5:21-26}

♦ Application comes out of a Changed life. And leads to a life transformed!
♦ What must I do to make God's Word real in me? What is my response?
♦ When will it end up in my day planner?
♦ Mediate over the passage

ASK YOURSELF THESE FIVE QUESTIONS:

♦ What illustration can I use to remember?
♦ How does the truth apply to my life?
♦ What is my personal prayer regarding these truths?
♦ What changes/improvements could I make in light of the truth?
♦ How should I carry out these changes?
♦ **Pray** to ask God how to implement His truth to you. Tell Others. Accountability.

STEP VII: MAKE USE OF THE BOOK CHART

♦ Write down what God is saying to you and what you have discovered and learned. By doing this, it will allow you to apply it to your life better!

"You can do it!"

Keep this guide "tucked" in your Bible for reference and guidance.

From: "Into Thy Word" C 2000 R.J. Krejcir

APPENDIX F

"Philosophy of Christian Education and Leadership"

The Marks of A Mature Believer:

The mark of a mature Christian is found in the process of total surrender! For us to grow, we must surrender our will, desires, plans upon our Lord Jesus Christ. Like driving a car in a strange unfamiliar area, with Christ as a passenger, we as human beings spend most of the time arguing, complaining, and debating the destination. Yet, we do not have a clue on where we are going. If, we allow Christ to get into the driver's seat, He will be able to take us around where we could never have gone before. And, if we sign over the Pink Slip to our Lord Jesus Christ, then He will take us to places that our most wild imaginations could ever fathom.

Thoughts on Christian Maturity:

a) The hub of the Christian life is Jesus Christ. (Colossians 3:4)
   We must have a firm, forward and moving commitment and trust in His work. (Romans 12:1, Galatians 2:20, Philippians 1:20-21);

b) The believer has support from other mature believers (John 15:5, Matthew 28:20);

c) Has purpose, direction, and filled with Christ's power (Ephesians 3:20, Philippians 4:13, Romans 12:1-2);

d) Is discipled in the gifts of the spirit (I Corinthians 12).

These four principles are the vehicle of our faith and the road in which we drive is the world in which we live. It is up to us to follow the navigation by the will of our Lord. We do this with recognition, response, and reliance upon Christ.

As with any vehicle, we need daily tune-ups:

Word of God (Matthew 4:4, I Peter 2:2)
Prayer and praise (Philippians 4:4-7, Colossians 3:16-17)
Love (I Corinthians 13, Mark 12:28-34, John 3:16)
Fellowship (John 13:34-35, I Corinthians 12:12-21, Ephesians 4:15-16)

All this equals the love and obedience we give out of our response of gratitude to what our Lord has done for us!

In Christ, all that comes to us is for God's glory, purpose, and our good (Romans 8:28). He seeks to bring us closer to Himself by His love, joy, and peace (Romans 5:1-5) that we may share His love with those around us to convey God's purpose for His people (John 17:20-24, Acts 2:24, 44-47).

I believe we should focus on the relational aspect of God and His unfathomable love for us, along side solid doctrine. To which this love is totally undeserved. We have a God that is real, is there for us, who knows us, and our lives matter to him. From this, we can know Him for eternity.

Some Thoughts on the Characteristics of a Leader:

a) A strong sense of vision and purpose (Philippians 3:10-14, Colossians 1:28-29);

b) Knowledge and experience (I Timothy 4:15-16, Romans 12:6-8);

c) Ability to attract and energize people (Colossians 4:7ff);

d) Perpetual learners (Philippians 4:8-9);

e) Persistence (Hebrews 12:1-3, II Timothy 2);

f) Spiritual and emotional maturity (II Corinthians 4:16-18, Philippians 1:12ff);

g) Love their work (I Thessalonians 2:8);

h) A risk taker (Matthew 25:16-30);

i) No fear of failure (Luke 22:31, Philippians 4:13);

j) Good followers (I Corinthians 11:1, Matthew 20:24); and

k) Good Listeners (James 1:19)

A Big Idea for your Churches discipleship of its high school people:

Mentoring: Train and facilitate programs of older adults helping with younger people, such as: Older high school students helping with elementary and junior high; College and young adults helping with the high school students; and, Older adults helping in all age categories as primary care givers and disciplers.

a) Have a vision and a plan;

b) Follow through with training and encouragement;

c) Provide extra events and socials for multigenerational gatherings.

d Matthew 28:16-20, Romans 12, I Corinthians 12, Galatians 6:1-10, Mark 1:35 B 2:12. These passages tell us discipleship and mentoring are not an option, but a command. We must follow out of our obedience and mentor in a multigenerational lifestyle, caring for the total person. It will move us from just prayer to prayer with care.

e) John 1:36-52, Acts 10:10. Maturity rose out of webs of relationships of older people interacting and discipling the younger.

f) Acts 11-15 tell us leadership is about discipleship as Barnabas was with Paul.

g) The Gospels tell us the model Jesus used were mentoring and small groups.

h) John 15 tells us discipling and mentoring are a lifestyle of personal dedication by our obedience; that we see people being taught and equipped to live for Christ: physically, mentally, socially, emotionally, as well as spiritually.

APPENDIX G

"How to lead a person to Christ:"

{Billy Graham / Bill Bright four-step process}

Step one: God's purpose, peace, and love. God wants you to experience peace and life abundantly and eternally (Romans 5:1, John 3:16, 10:10).

Step Two: Our problem: Separation. God created us in His own image to have abundant life. He did not make us robots to automatically love and obey Him but gave us the gift of free choice. Hence, we chose to disobey God on our own will, which resulted in our separation (Romans 3:23, 6:23).

Our attempts through the ages have failed to bridge the gap (Isaiah 59:2, Proverbs 14:12).

Step Three: God's remedy: The cross. Jesus Christ is the only answer to this problem. He died on the cross, rose from the grave, and paid our penalty (I Timothy 2:5, I Peter 3:18, Romans 5:8).

Step Four: Our Response. To receive Christ, we must trust in Him by personal invitation (Revelation 3:20, John 1:12, Romans 10:9).

Then pray with the individual and make sure they receive discipling. And focus on the basics, which include prayer, scripture, devotional life, accountability, and discipleship.

Priorities: We should seek a church that is growing in Jesus Christ in three priorities:

First, worship, praise and study (Philippians 3:10).

Second, growing in a relationship with other believers and discipleship (Matthew 5:23, Proverbs 17:17).

Third, reaching our friends, neighbors, and the world (Matthew 28, Genesis 12:1-3).

EPILOGUE

I Hear and I forget.
I see and I remember. I
do and I understand.

(Ancient Chinese Proverb)

Afterword

Psalm 119

For the director of music. A psalm of David. The heavens declare the glory of God; the skies proclaim the work of his hands. Day after day they pour forth speech; night after night they display knowledge. There is no speech or language where their voice is not heard. Their voice goes out into all the earth, their words to the ends of the world. In the heavens he has pitched a tent for the sun, which is like a bridegroom coming forth from his pavilion, like a champion rejoicing to run his course. It rises at one end of the heavens and makes its circuit to the other; nothing is hidden from its heat. The law of the LORD is perfect, reviving the soul. The statutes of the LORD are trustworthy, making wise the simple. The precepts of the LORD are right, giving joy to the heart. The commands of the LORD are radiant, giving light to the eyes. The fear of the LORD is pure, enduring forever. The ordinances of the LORD are sure and altogether righteous. They are more precious than gold, than much pure gold; they are sweeter than honey, than honey from the comb. By them is your servant warned; in keeping them there is great reward. Who can discern his errors? Forgive my hidden faults. Keep your servant also from willful sins; may they not rule over me. Then will I be blameless, innocent of great transgression. May the words of my mouth and the meditation of my heart be pleasing in your sight, O LORD, my Rock and my Redeemer.

ABOUT THE AUTHOR

Richard Joseph Krejcir, pastor, teacher, speaker is a graduate of Fuller Theological Seminary in Pasadena California and has amounted nearly 20 years of pastoral ministry experience mostly in youth ministry, including serving as a church growth consultant. He is married and is serving in a church in Southern California.

Printed in the United States
24838LVS00003B/8